Love, Laughter, And Living

Receiving and Sharing Poems from the Heart

Joan Pace Kennedy

PUBLISHED by PARABLES
Earthly Stories with a Heavenly Meaning

Joan Pace Kennedy

Dedication

This book is dedicated with love to my husband of 52 years, Jay, and all our "J" children: Juanette, Jackie, Jeffery, and Justin.

Title: Love, Laughter, And Living
Creator(s):Joan Pace Kennedy

All Rights Reserved
Copyriight: July, 2016
ISBN 978-1-945698-02-6

Published By Parables
www.PublishedByParables.com

Foreword

The purpose of this book is to share words given the author. They evoke and elicit feelings. Some poems are short and whimsical while others are longer and thought provoking. Many use rhythm and rhyme to convey a message; some are simply words in motion.

Many of the poems included are the result of my life experiences and personal losses and blessings. They reflect the love of family, of literacy, and a personal relationship with God.

The words create a mood and appeal to the emotions. Many writings deal with self and feelings of pride, sadness, anger, happiness, and accomplishment, along with poems having a romantic flavor. Included are poems that make us smile, laugh out loud, or even cry.

There are poems that propose that old age and eventually death is nothing to be afraid of if we trust in the Lord and are optimistic. The realization of death and dying as a part of life brings other related poems.

"God has been good to me and I have been truly blessed. Whatever gift or talent I possess is a gift from God and I want to always give God the glory."

Joan Pace Kennedy

Acknowledgment

Many thanks go to my friends, peers, and fellow LRA members who have encouraged me for some time to share my writings.

A very special thank you goes to my extraordinary family...husband Jay, daughter Jackie, siblings, Elfie and Mike, and my grandchildren who believed in me and this endeavor. Their love, patience, and confidence are greatly appreciated.

I would also like to thank Dr. John Dee Jeffries and the staff at Parables Publishing for their help in bringing this book to completion.

And, last but not least, I give thanks for the influence of these exceptional people who have already gone to their heavenly home: my mom and dad, Betty and Winfred Dutch Pace, and my three children, Juanette, Jeffery, and Justin. I was blessed to have them in my life and they will always occupy a place in my heart.

-Joan Pace Kennedy

Preface

As a wife, mother, and educator Joan Kennedy has lived her life as though she were a village fountain, ceaselessly pouring forth, a life of continuous giving. After 36 years of service as an educator, it would be reasonable to think that she had given all there was to give. Yet, Joan has poured forth once again, giving us a collection of poems in her own honest and unpretentious voice, reflective of her own real life experiences, expressing the joy and the values and the beliefs that have guided her all these years. I loved reading Love, Laughter, and Living, and I hope you will, too. It's an impressive body of work.

-- Brod Bagert

''Brod Bagert is the award-winning author of 17 books of poetry for children, young-adults, and adults. Born and raised in New Orleans, Brod married his high-school sweetheart, practiced law, served in public office, and reared four children. In 1992, Brod closed his twenty-one year law practice and became one of America's very few full-time, professional poets. Brod continues to live in New Orleans with his wife Debby, where they spend quality time with their children and grandchildren.''

Joan Pace Kennedy

Contents

I. Home and Family......7

II. Literacy and Learning......39

III. Community and Country......69

IV. Faith and Friends......95

V. Love and Laughter......131

VI. Holidays and Happiness......151

VII. Along the Way......173

Chapter 1
Home and Family

Dirt to Dirt
Memory Moments
Who Am I?
Justin, My Justin
Without Him
Mom and Dad
Golden Memories
My Dad
Happy Mother's Day
My Mom
My Sister
This is the Day
Daddy's Hands
The Hour of Death
Family Portrait
Home is Where the Heart Is
Remembering

Joan Pace Kennedy

Dirt to Dirt

     The deal is made, the deed is done
      What was the father's is now his son's
The fertile earth warmed by the sun
Embraces the feelings of the father's son.

      Bought in forty-two and cleared by hand
      Broke by the sweat and power of the man
      He would raise his son to love this land
      And be proud when ownership passed to his hand.

Like a map he traces over furrow and hill
Recalling, remembering, and it seems that still
Sometimes he can yet hear across the field
His father's voice and to it he'd yield.

      Work was hard and many days forlorn
      There were no short rows on this cotton farm
      The boys and girls worked side by side
      They loved their land and their father's pride.

The first bale of cotton to arrive at the gin
Was the goal to meet and then the father would grin
When handed his bonus above payment due
Then the boys got overalls and new pairs of shoes.

That new John Deere tractor plowed late into the night
An excited young man who just wanted to drive
This powerful machine and he glowed in his pride
For the love of his land and this tractor to ride.

> The smell of the freshly turned plowed-open dirt
> The feel of the sun through his unbuttoned shirt
> A farm-boy at heart with a love for outdoors
> Don't fence him in with the walls and the floors.

Joan Pace Kennedy

Memory Moments

Like a rerun from the past
Flickering across my memory screen
Frames with scenes of long ago.

    A little girl watching for Daddy
    Sitting outside on the front porch
    Waiting patiently for her hero.

Playing dress-up dolls with sister
Singing as she picked out
Melodies on the old piano.

    Taking care of baby brother
    Trying to be a guardian angel
    Shielding him from hurt and sorrow.

    Across the USA by car
    Family vacations near and far
    Never worrying about tomorrow.

A single parent family at home
While Daddy worked construction
Surviving without our mentor.

Reading books, going to school
Meeting people and making friends
Continuing to mature and grow.

Memories strong with ties that bind
Fill my mental video screen
Then the scenes rewind once more.

    Family…with its members close
    As pages in a book
    That I read over and over and over.

Joan Pace Kennedy

Who Am I?

My heavenly Father formed me;
He made me from the start
My mother gave birth to me
and carried me close to her heart.

    My daddy raised me with love and discipline
    Mama lovingly taught me right from wrong.
Family taught me lots of lessons, how to get along

    Sharing, working and playing together,
    most times singing a song.
        Teachers guided and mentored me,
        as I absorbed much in school

The pastor preached as we all learned to follow
the Golden Rule.

My hard-working husband
showed me love, strength, and comfort
    Long hours away from home
        in order to provide for our family.

I nurtured my own children
and they loved and respected me
    Though they thought I was somewhat mean
    and tough at times.

Entrusted in my care, students looked up to me as well
In the classroom,
    I tried to prepare them with lessons for their lives.

    "The last of life for which the first was made..."
        Those familiar words of a poem
    However, it has now come down to that part for me
        The last, however long it turns out to be.

I do not want my life gone with my headstone reading,
"She came...She went"
I want my life to have meaning and substance...a life well spent
I want to have touched a life; I want to have made a difference
    I want someone to know I cared. I want to be remembered
    as a loving wife.

    I want my children to have memories of a mom whose life
centered around them...
    But, I want them also to remember me...as one who wanted
    To be of service, accomplish things, and leave a positive
influence.

        Who am I? I'm me, a woman, just one individual
        A wife first of all, then a mother to four
        Grandmother to five, then great-grandma to five more.

Who am I? Someone who has seen happy days and sad ones
Nevertheless, I have been abundantly blessed.
    The good in my life has far outweighed the bad
And when my time comes, I'm prepared and ready for my end.

Who am I? Someone who came and someone who went
But, someone who did a lot of "going" and "doing" in between.

Joan Pace Kennedy

Justin, My Justin

Justin my son, Justin a man
Oh how the Air Force has changed you
Lanky and thin, you stand straight and tall
Projecting an Airman image to all.

      Justin grown up and gone for sure
      From the realm of my out stretched arms
      No longer needing me near
      Oh, my son, how time does fly!

   You refused to stay little quite long enough
   Those early years crammed with all sorts of stuff
   Like tractors and toys, skateboard and bikes
   From "hulk-pants" to jams, and jeans fitting tight.

Justin my Justin, where did my boy go
Recollections fade as I try to remember you so
   That little round face with cheeks so full
   And the voice that asked, "Mama, ain't I been good?"

      My tough little tiger, though tender at heart
      Trying at times, now have NO doubt.
      You were rough and rowdy, at times just loud
      But you were never consumed with following the crowd.

Love, Laughter And Living

You did things your way, sometimes angrily
Often aloof, not taking a part.
In making new friends, you sometimes stood back
A little quiet, reserved, until your plan was hatched.

    Always striving to do your best
        You always made us proud with your scores
Changing schools proved to be fun and good
Bringing revelations buckling down you would.

And so you did and dug right in
The numbers started to fall in place
Fear of failure now far behind
You prepared to graduate, seventh in line.

      In Kindergarten cutting another child's hair
      And in first grade staying in at recess to draw.
      Justin my child, where did you go,
      From the little boy of so long ago?

    Now the years are spent, eighteen are gone
    The man in blue is the little boy grown
    Wonder shines from your eyes so blue
Remember well my son, how mother loves you!

Joan Pace Kennedy

Without Him

Out of my darkness I cry
Where are you?
        I cannot see. I reach but there is only a void.

Out of my hurt, I sense life going on
But what about me
        I feel like I'm melting…slowly fading away.

        No longer the same, I am broken
        Like a puzzle with an essential piece missing
        I am forever incomplete.

I search my mind, trying to remember
Your face, your smile, your being
But you are so distant.

        Why did you go?
        I slide back to that fateful evening
        Etched forever in my memory.

In my darkness, I realize the dreadful reality
I sense the finality
        I grieve for the loss.

Love, Laughter And Living

Out of my darkness is the light of your memory
A ray to brighten my day
    And help me endure the night.

        Only when I look up can I feel release
          Of the ache, the agony, the sorrow
      You are up and with that knowledge, I go on.

Where are you? I search and then I remember
You were here and so you will always be
      Love does not end, it cannot be taken away.

      Where there is breadth and depth and height
      Love soars above all else
          And encircles those left.

Joan Pace Kennedy

Mom and Dad

That big old house no longer stands
Down the road beneath the giant oak tree
      And from that place are also gone
            Those two held so dear to me.

Dear grey-haired mom with apron tied
Around her cotton print dress
      Never complained of the hard times
        Although she often endured so much stress.

And in memory I can almost see
My dad as he sits by the fireplace
His pipe held tight between his teeth
      A twinkle in his eye, a smile on his face.

      Parents of twelve stretched over the years
      Four girls and the other, eight boys
When holidays and reunion time came
Just imagine the gathering and the noise.

The crowded room filled with happy people
Eating and drinking coffee or tea
Swapping stories and telling tall tales
Everyone laughing with glee.

Love, Laughter And Living

    It was easy to tell the center of attention
Dad, smoking his old pipe with ease
        Surrounded by loving family members
           His grandchildren on his knees.

Never a dull moment with the Kennedy clan
             Standing around or backed up to the fire
        Visits were fun, a fruit basket turnover
        When someone got up, he lost his chair.

But then they were gone and the house stood bare
Until fire wiped all traces away
        Nothing can erase those yesteryears
            They are in my memory to stay.

Joan Pace Kennedy

Golden Memories

    Golden memories of another time
Of an ageless couple housed at Pine
            From first day wed they forged ahead
                To build a life together.

Their union was blessed with children four
Three survive, one is no more
            Life was filled with songs galore
              As they lived a life together.

Family, church, Eastern Star, and the Lodge
Friends and community services
            All rolled continuously into one
              As they met their goals together.

Taking hold of the helm, steering straight
Sights set on things above
            Love and laughter filled the house
              As they shared a life together.

So many memories span the mind
But suffice it to say for sure
            This couple from Pine, these parents of mine,
Provided a home safe and secure
              As they raised their family together.

My Dad

Though short in stature, he stands tall
His face against the wind.
      He's worked many a day for too little pay
          But he still can wear a grin.

            This man is proud, yet humble inside
              He's seen times both happy and sad.
He's loving, gentle, warm, and good
This man whom I call Dad.

      He's a natural born leader, a giant of a man
          Responsibility he shoulders with ease.
            He's not afraid to stand and be counted
For the things in which he believes.

If you give him a task, he'll see it through
For his word is certainly his bond.
            In his community and in his church
      He's one of whom people have grown quite fond.

His friends are many both far and wide
He's traveled and met quite a few
      Through the I.B.E.W. and the D.A.V.
           Masonic Lodge and Eastern Star too.

Joan Pace Kennedy

Dad's always been there to lend a hand
And I'm so very proud to say
His guidance, love, and counsel
Helped make me what I am today!

Love, Laughter And Living

Happy Mother's Day

    Mother's Day seems an appropriate time
To say thank you for all you've done
        To help make us who we are today
Two daughters and a son.

You've always been there to lend a hand
        To believe in us and understand.
            With love you guided us through the years
Nurtured, supported, and dried our tears.

Now, mother dear, just know for sure
We love you in a special way.
        So we take this means of saying to you
A happy happy Mother's Day!

Joan Pace Kennedy

My Mom

Born in Bogalusa in the warm month of June
Betty was the youngest girl in a family of ten.
        The baby daughter of Newt and Leoda
        Raised near Crain's Creek on Duncan hill.

She played and sang with her sisters on the porch
Caught the eye of many young men.
        But the one who finally won Bet's hand
Was a handsome guy named Dutch from Pine.

Betty dropped out of school and became his wife
    Then a mother to four children, one died early in life.
A Parish FHA and Cub Scout Den Mother was she
    All the while cooking and sewing for her own family.

        Eastern Star, Bible Class, and Home Demonstration
        Church and Singing School filled her busy life.
    She kept the fires burning when hubby worked away
Kids "spit shined and polished" welcomed Dad home.

You could always count on Betty to be on the phone
To check on the deaths, those sick and shut in
    She'd whip up and deliver an egg pie for those
    Who were terminally ill or for someone bedridden.

Love, Laughter And Living

A stoic woman, this lady's been called
Her trust in God was evident
    A breast cancer survivor and supporter of causes
        Betty's positive attitude spoke volumes.

Betty was known for her generous nature
For her love of music and song
For loving care of friends and neighbors around her
    And sharing their grief in great times of loss.

Betty was quite proud of her entire family
    Those two girls, her son, and the grandchildren
    But the love of her life was that man by her side
        With whom she shared more than sixty years.

Joan Pace Kennedy

My Sister

I don't remember the day of her birth
For in October I was not yet two.
But I do recall the many days hence
When, together, all sorts of things we'd do.

We played in the yard, climbed the chinaberry tree
Cut out paper dolls, read books from the library
Sang around the piano as she played out loud
Traveled and sang to many a church crowd.

We shared a room, a closet, a bed
For eighteen years, until the day I wed.
I was the eldest, the oldest of three
A baby brother, my sister, and me.

Sisters are special, all down through time
Sharing times of joy and times of crying.
Ears to listen to each other's woes
And share exciting tales of dates and beaus.

My sister was younger, the one in the middle
But she was older than the baby boy.
That middle child often feels left out
Older ones get things first and the baby gets his way.

Love, Laughter And Living

We sisters attended the same country school
        Both shared teachers as we went through the grades
        Participated in sports, stage plays, and such
            Each, in her own way, an individual.

Sisters we were and sisters we are
            Closer today now than ever
Sisters who travel and enjoy special times
        Spent together shopping and in LRA.

Joan Pace Kennedy

This is the Day

This is the day that the Lord has made
And He made you for me
So let's love like there's no tomorrow
And not worry about what might be.

We have so much going for us
        On this day as well as before
This is the day that the Lord has made
        Come let me love you a little more.

I remember the day that you told me
        I do, and then I was your wife
              And we pledged our love forever
                  To be one as we shared our life.

This is the day that the Lord has made
Come walk with your hand in mine
        Just promise our love will grow stronger
Endure and stand the test of time.

Oh glorious day that the Lord has made
    As I look into your eyes
        May He bless our love forever
        Until that day comes we die.

This is the day that the Lord has made
And He made you for me
        So let's love like there's no tomorrow
Not worry about things yet to be.

        Our union was made in heaven
        I thank Him each day from my heart
And I silently vow as I gaze at you now
    Until our death, we never will part.

Joan Pace Kennedy

Daddy's Hands

Soft and gentle hands cradled me with kindness
their strength instilled a sense of safety and security
as they sought to soothe many childhood sufferings.

Patient hands were helpful as I learned to ride a bike,
watchful and wary when I began to drive and
seriously structured when I needed guidance.

Generous hands open in giving to those less fortunate
steadfastly provided the needs of family and home
and proved to have our best interests at heart.

Capable hands could tape and fix almost anything broken
this meant we didn't have to go out and buy new
nor wait in line for costly repairs.

Skilled hands that maneuvered the car and drove for miles
on vacations, exposed us to the wonders of the country
and left us with memories that nothing can erase.

Camping hands, happy as they unfolded and pitched the tent
pulled out the green Coleman stove
and fried bacon in the cool mountain air.

Loving hands held many surprises…toys, candy, and gifts
      even produced unexpected picnics
with cooking under a bridge by the creek.
Exhausted hands, after putting in a long day's labor
      tanned and tempered from toiling
      were never too tired to give us a tender hug.

Talented hands, trained to twist wire and connect electricity
      were calloused and worn from years of wear
          but committed to be a leader and an example.

Hands that motioned and moved as he moderated meetings
    honest hands, determined to be fair and impartial
revealed a man of integrity.

Reverent hands were humble as he held the Bible
      stood to give the devotion on "Love" or
sat and took minutes, a record of church services.

           Veteran hands, the right one over his heart
as he gave the pledge or stood in homage
      exhibited patriotism for his country.

Hands spotted, mottled with age, strength waning
      tried, with difficulty, to open a sealed lid
      or grip a handle to keep from falling.

Wrinkled and weathered hands, weak with age
        trembled from the results of cancer treatments
          faced the unknown with unwavering faith.

Hands heavy in a coma…hot, swollen, and inert
        I held them gently, held on dearly
        trying to ward off the inevitable.

Joan Pace Kennedy

Hands, cold and still in death, now folded in rest
with wedding and Masonic rings in view
    those hands reflected a man of character…
        husband,
            father,
                brother,
                      friend.

The Hour of Death

We knew his death was imminent
We'd been told the end was near
But to hover at the bedside
And whisper in hopes he hears
Is an eerie kind of feeling
A scene in every sense, surreal.

We were there, his wife and three children
Others, too, with their love and zeal
But we weren't prepared for his leaving.
No, we were not ready at all.

We watched as the life was ebbing
And his warm pink skin turned pale
The swollen hands never moving
Dull blue replaced the color under his nails.

Daddy was always the strong one
He was the leader of our clan
Definitely the head of the household
The one who would always take a stand.
He made decisions with the aid of his wife
But it was he who led our family, all his life.

Joan Pace Kennedy

  He gave of himself to neighbors and kin
  He treasured his friendships with Masonic men.
Patriotic, this Army Veteran loved giving back.
Presented the graduation American Legion Award
    Put out and collected Memorial Day cemetery flags.
    He wanted Veterans honored on those special days.

Then the time came when he was gone
Life slipped away and then there was none.
  We sat there quietly
  Tears had been shed all along.
  Now we each touched his arm, his hand, his face
    And said good-bye to the life, now erased.

But nothing can mar the memories of life
Of the happy times spent with children and wife
  Of home and family, travel, and friends
  Of church and singing, fishing and such
Memories to suffice us when we miss him so much.
    Daddy is gone, but he'll always be here.

We see him, we hear him, as we remember his words.
  Although gone in body, he'll always live on in spirit.

Family Portrait

In a cottage nestled in the pines
Lived a couple whose life was love entwined.

He was tall, blonde, and tan
This handsome, rugged, hard-working man.
    She with dark hair and eyes of blue
    They shared their love faithful and true.

        They traveled over the nation wide
        This country boy and his devoted bride
They shared the good times and the bad
Had happy days, though some were sad.

    To them were born children four
    One for a single day, no more.
The other three grew fine and fair
    One sandy blonde and two dark haired.

This family shared life to the height
Loved each other with all their might
    Pulled and struggled and sometimes fought
    But, always together, never for naught.

Joan Pace Kennedy

Paradise, they called their home
And although they often from it roamed
To work pipeline across the USA
This family traveled, but never to stay.
Made new friends from far and wide
Crossing the plains and mountain sides
      Over rocky hills and into valleys low
      Very few states to which they did not go.

To be able to view such a vast expanse
That not everyone is offered the chance
      Was a blessing from God they did appreciate
          Gave thanks to Him for whatever their fate.

Life was bountiful, rich, and sweet
Thank God this man and woman did meet
      To join their lives and share such love
      That only comes from heaven above.

Home is Where the Heart Is

Home is where the heart is
    A place of eternal love and trust
        A shelter from the storms of life
            With arms open to console and comfort,

Home is the center of family affection
        The hub around which activity revolves
            The socket of its extended arms
        And always the focus of the network..

    Home is the constant gathering point
    For all the birds who have flown the coop
Disseminated though they all may be
They still come home to roost.

Home is a place of warm abode
Where feelings of coziness fill the air
    And a sense of contentment and satisfaction
    Reigns without our knowing why.

    Home is much more than just a dwelling
        More than walls, a roof, and floor
Home is the core of our existence
    Our true being reverts to something more.

Wonderful home, that comfortable niche
Where pieces come together, as in a puzzle
Each his own person, solid and whole
Though not complete until united.

Joan Pace Kennedy

Remembering...

    The sands of time have moved along
        But our life as we knew it is gone.
We face each day, cope best we can
        But without you here, we're at a loss.

Our son first, and then our daughter
Too soon, we said good-bye.
        But, you'll live forever in memory
            As we tell our stories, laugh, and cry.

            Remembering you two is easy
            Recalling the way you smiled
      Your quick wit and smart retorts
Keep you always alive in our hearts.

      Life does continue, we all must go on
      What choice do we have down here?
But knowing now, where both of you are
        Gives reason, through grace, to persevere.

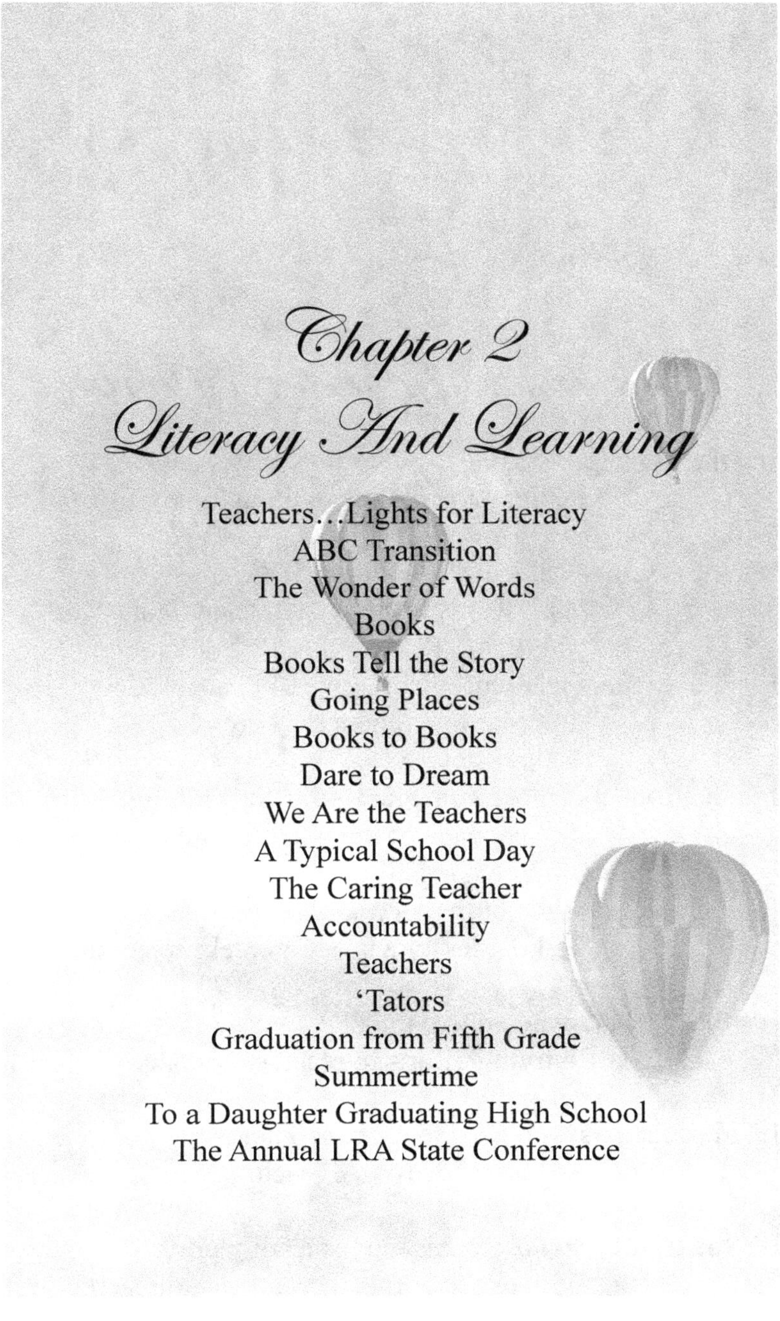

Chapter 2
Literacy And Learning

Teachers…Lights for Literacy
ABC Transition
The Wonder of Words
Books
Books Tell the Story
Going Places
Books to Books
Dare to Dream
We Are the Teachers
A Typical School Day
The Caring Teacher
Accountability
Teachers
'Tators
Graduation from Fifth Grade
Summertime
To a Daughter Graduating High School
The Annual LRA State Conference

Joan Pace Kennedy

Teachers... Lights for Literacy

It's the teachers who daily impart bits of wisdom
        Helping to enlighten young minds.

It's the teachers who go that extra mile
        With words firm, yet gentle and kind.

It's the teachers who unselfishly give of themselves
        In order that others may grow.

It's the teachers whose strategies guide the children
        So that each of them learns and knows.

It's the teachers who burn that midnight oil
        Making lesson plans for weeks to come.

It's the teachers who adhere to IEPs
        In trying efforts to reach every one.

It's the teachers who use the set benchmarks
        As they endeavor to teach.

It's the teachers whose goals move steadily upward
        With expectations for students to reach.

It's the teachers whose paths the students will follow
>   While trying to grasp the concept line.

It's the teachers who they will long remember
>   Even after the passage of time.

Clearly, it's the teachers who are the lights of the world
>   For without their teaching…
>   >   We'd have no more teachers
>   >   >   No doctors, no lawyers, or such.

Like the simple message beaming from bumper stickers
>   >   If you can read…
>   You owe a teacher so much.

Literacy is a light that is daily lit
>   By teachers throughout the world.

So hold you light high if you're a teacher
>   For you've touched
>   >   The life of many a boy and girl.

Joan Pace Kennedy

ABC Transition

Magical alphabet letters

Creating powerful words

Grouped into meaningful sentences

Building intriguing paragraph

Rolled into countless chapters

Culminating in an unforgettable book

That touches endless souls

Changing lives forever

Leaving its mark on humanity.

The Wonder of Words

Words –the sheer beauty of their audible sound
    Printed texts, words we read
    Books and stories written down.

Words – rhythmic sounds that stir the soul
    Oral stories so aptly told
    Legends passed on from long ago.

Words – retrieving scenes from depths of the mind
    Descriptions of other places and times
    Projecting images of folklore and rhyme.

Words - made up of letters from the alphabet
    Creations of vowel and consonant mix
    Skillfully shuffled to make them all fit.

Words - a record of emotions, full of desire
    To stretch the imagination wide
    Such stories bridge gaps or perhaps turn tides.

Words - softly whispered or fitly spoken
    Provide encouragement, comfort, and leaven
    To those for whom the words are given.

Words - a legacy of feelings, visual imagery
    Echoed aloud or etched in stone
    Syllables once spoken, never gone.

Joan Pace Kennedy

Books

Without good books, the world's a bore
      But with them you will grow
            The printed pages
            Down through the ages
    Have kept education aglow.

    Schools and books are synonymous
   We think of them one and the same
Instructors there teach us to read
Then on books we begin to feed
     Until we know all the classics by name.

    Books are like friends to treasure and hold
        To care for and use every day
            They offer so much
             Just reach out and touch
    And soon you will be on your way.

    Books open doors to worlds beyond
      Our normal realm of existence
Travel to the stars
    To the moon or Mars
        Reading provides the building suspense.

With a book we can be whatever we choose
As each day we fulfill a need
        Become a doctor, politician, or lawyer
           Aviator, actor, merchant, or teacher
    The books available are endless indeed.

      Pursue a career, follow your dream
        Let books be a part of your day
Take time to read
        Then read with speed
           Let nothing stand in your way.

Books are vehicles in which to travel
All over the world so wide
      To see the pyramids in Egypt grand
         The snow-covered Alps of Switzerland
            Or Spain and its countryside.

           Let books be your magic carpet
          On which you journey through time.
    Experience the future as well as the past
A lifetime is short, it goes by too fast
    Not to read and develop your mind.

Joan Pace Kennedy

Books Tell the Stories

Books tell the stories of three pigs and three bears
Goldilocks ate porridge
and broke one of the chairs.
Red Riding Hood walked to grandmother's with care
But that sly, cunning wolf
was already there.
Three Billy Goats Gruff tripped over the bridge
And finally made it
to the grass on the ridge.
The race between the hare and the tortoise was won
By that slow plodding turtle
showing it could be done.
Cinderella kept house and around the fireplace cleaned
Her stepmother and stepsisters
were, to Cinderella, so mean.
The princess proved surely she was of royal descent
By discerning the pea
under a mattress stack spent.
Tall tales of Paul Bunyan, his big ox, Babe, too
Share arenas with Pecos Bill
and his beloved Lightfoot Sue.
Chicken Little thought the sky was falling and ran to warn

Love, Laughter And Living

The farmer, and following her
were other animals on the farm.
Snow White and the dwarfs, from seven down to one
Create a warm caring story
full of laughter and lots of fun.
The Little Red Hen, such an industrious feathered fowl
Did plant, harvest, mill, and bake
with no help from the outside crowd.
Deep in the forest, Hansel and Gretel were left alone
Danger lurked as they nibbled
candy from the sweet covered home.
Anansi, the spider, used his wits to outsmart his friends
A tiny trickster, this mischief-maker
was triumphant beginning to end.
The shoemaker was poor, by no fault of his own
Surprised was he to find new shoes
made by elves before the dawn.
John Henry, a steel-driving man,
left his mark upon the land
He beat that steam engine before he died
a hammer in his hand.
Out the window went the beans,
the ones brought home that day
Jack awoke to find a beanstalk
growing tall, up skyward way.
All these stories come magically alive
When we open up the book
and read the words inside.
The stories live on, not just on the pages
But in our hearts and minds vivid
for ages through repetition and retelling.
Books, books, and more books…
they tell the everlasting stories
We read, retell,
and remember.

Joan Pace Kennedy

Going Places

Going, going, going, gone
 Moving, traveling, wherever we roam
There's a world of reading along the way
We read as we travel each and every day.

Whether near or far, west or east
We'll find words on which our eyes will feast
 Discover road signs, and names all around
As we roll down the highways, ease through little towns.

 Words on the billboards that line city streets
 Logos for places to stop, gas, and eat
 Golden arches formed by the giant letter M
And lighted letters beckon come rest at the inn.

The radio blares words, jingles, and songs
The sign by the church reads come and belong
 A tall marquee sign flashes a public note
 Gives the time and the temp for those on the road.

 Those who can read numbers, symbols, and words
 Interpret signs and understand what they have heard
 The ability to read, such an important feat
Helps us make sense of what we see, what we eat.

Reading provides escape when we've nothing to do
Curl up with a book and soon we'll be through
    Going places we've dreamed of, never been to before
        Seeing people and things and oh so much more.

        Exciting distant places, we'll go visit and then
      Take out our book and open again
A variety of books to experience, enjoy
Writing unique for each girl and each boy.

    Books give us friends from the pages we read
      Good books and good friends, a good pair indeed
Books give us wings, they open the doors
Encourage us to read, in a chair, on the floor.

    On our magic carpet, books inspire us to fly
      Enable us to soar through those times now gone by
As we travel through pages, the words come to life
        Going, going, gone…we read through our flight.

Joan Pace Kennedy

Dare to Dream

Imagine your dreams
Visualize yourself in the future
Devise a plan and maneuver changes
To dream is to thrive, mature, and grow.

Without your dreams
Expectations dry up, evaporate, and disappear
Set priorities, remain disciplined and dedicated
Plan well to avoid pitfalls and allow for detours.

Support your dreams
Set long range goals and strive toward the mark
Take calculated risks, always with a purpose
Stretch your limit and make sacrifices.

Encourage your dreams
Train to be ready to run with high expectations
Be passionate, responsible, devoted
Pace yourself and go the distance.

Follow your dreams
Though difficult, be persistent and diligent
Enhance and experience freedom

Be committed and forge ahead with enthusiasm.

Chase your dreams
Take heed and express your individualism
With determination and perseverance
Go for the long run, be passionate and endure.

Fulfill your dreams
Establish a mission, choose a direction
Invest time wisely and stay connected
Be a dream chaser and pursue steadfastly.

Dare to dream
Take aim, focus and launch upward, skyward
Make your journey worthwhile
Blast off like a rocket and soar like an eagle.

Joan Pace Kennedy

Books to Books

Whenever we're born we do not know
Just what we'll do, or where we'll go
At the end of that year, my mom gave birth
And that began my journey on earth.

A little country girl who lived out of town
Who found it easier to smile than frown
Surrounded by family and friends as well
My life story's happy and not hard to tell.

Those great early teachers who cast the mold
They taught me much in those days of old
Threw out the challenge to learn and grow
I never dreamed how far I could go.

They set the stage, role models all
I left with zeal to answer the call
To become an educator, to share, to reach
To dare to enter the field to teach.

Years of college and then some more
An elementary teacher for just over a score
Then back for hours to gain certification

A school librarian is now my vocation.
Books from the beginning, multiplied at the end
Printed words on pages – always my friends
Surrounded by books, I continue to smile
For books take me places across the vast miles.

Joan Pace Kennedy

We Are the Teachers

The school doors open, children rush in
We welcome and nurture, these the parents send
Ready for learning, for molding, and such
Needing pencils and paper, and structure so much.

Too soon we discover, not all learn the same
Some take a little longer, comprehension's the blame.
Differentiated instruction, try to reach every child
No Child Left Behind, proven methods and style.

Hold to the cutting edge, raise test scores we're told
Burn lots of midnight oil, turn gray and grow old.
Stay there in the trenches, work hard for low pay
And satisfaction of achievement at the end of the day.

Education's still the same, as ever it will be
New methods come and go; it's up to us to see
What works best for the ones entrusted to our care,
For teachers make the difference in learning everywhere.

Love, Laughter And Living

A Typical School Day

Arriving early,
I savor the silence until…Wham! Bam! Slam!
Here they come; the buses have arrived.
The hall is filled with bodies, loud voices much alive
As they hurry off to their rooms and rules
To begin another day at the elementary school.
Hold it now; what is that you say?
Do not push and shove; I am not in your way.
What's for breakfast this morning?
I need some toast, eggs, and things.
Have to go now…catch you later my friend
Nearly time for the bell and once classes begin
Reading First, that crucial 90 minute block,
No interruption, no watching the clock
Retelling the story, after they've read
So they know exactly what really was said.
The bell for recess, I hear its sound loud.
Get out of the way or be crushed by the crowd.
Technology time, all kids go to the Lab,
Sitting quietly at a computer monitor,
Fingers on the keyboard, pecking aloud.
They're creating a project, for others to see,

Perhaps on America, the land of the free.
Line up for lunch, walk to the cafeteria;
    Get hot foods from the line and milk from the cooler.
        Canteen waits with chips, candy, and treats.
       After lunch, how can one still find "room" to eat?
          The day is wearing on and the afternoon has come;
            Last periods of the day cannot be "hum drum".
       Get all excited, get adrenalin pumping
              Students gear up, information is coming.
             A typical day within the walls of a school
But, don't judge them all by this particular one.
    Every day is unique; it is never the same!
School changes each day, except for bodies and names!

Love, Laughter And Living

The Caring Teacher

I was disappointed with myself,
threatened with failure,
emotionally damaged and worn,

Void of motivation,
filled with terror,
until the inevitable happened.

A caring teacher with affirmation
armed with positive ideas
helped me learn from my mistakes.

Now, the bend in the road
leads to higher planes
as together we struggle to grow.

An obvious change has been duly noted
life is full of expectations
still making mistakes, I continue to learn.

That teacher, the equation's essential part
prepared and accountable she came
and that has made all the difference.

Joan Pace Kennedy

Accountability

Accountability, oh what an awesome word
To know that we're responsible for
What students have seen and heard.

Our daily lesson plans with pride
For years we all have done
Had written goals and objectives
And even had some fun.

Now strict standards and staunch benchmarks
From the state are handed down
Portfolio assessment and records abound.

Will our students really gain and grow
From these strategies oh so new
Well, it's all up to the teachers
The ones like me and you.

Teachers

It's hard to love every child
When some are noisy and loud
And some are dirty, soiled, and grimy
While others stand out in the crowd.

It's hard to love every child
All shapes, and sizes, and forms
But each is an individual
Look out for his and her charms.

Every child needs a part of you
To guide and lead their way
Help them become the best they can be
Make theirs a happy day!

Tators

She said we all are 'tators
In this world in which we live
    We choose which one we'll be
What we'll take and what we'll give.

Some come to be known as Dick
Dic-tators is what they are
    Like generals and lieutenants
    Heralding orders near and far.

Then some sit back and watch it all
    Spec-tators are their name
        Observing while the things get done
But have no action in the game.

Of course, there are always agi-tators
    They feel the need to stir
While others work and strive toward goals
    They move within with burrs.

The hesi-tators wait and see
        They pause, procrastinate
Stay on the sidelines uninvolved
    Until it's much too late.

Love, Laughter And Living

The imi-tators try to be
Like some person in the room
    They pattern after someone
        With a smile or filled with gloom.

    And then, there's that poor 'tator
        Who has "nair-ee" a dime
    He's always short on money
And can't find any time.

    Too busy when you ask him
    To help or give some aid
        Involved in personal endeavors
    He's quick to leave the stage.

We need some medi-tators
        Who'll think, and then use the means
    For only with thought and action
Can we accomplish goals and dreams.

    Everyone's an edu-tator
    In this world in which we live
There's wonder on this great blue marble
    Take less and more you'll give.

Joan Pace Kennedy

Graduation from Fifth Grade

The time has come, the year is gone
You'll leave grade school
Which you've called home
From Kindergarten up through fifth grade.

Only yesterday, it seems, you were a child
And now, today, things are different
You sit anxiously waiting in your chair
As my mind travels back in time.

Graduation is a rite of passage
Whether from fifth grade or twelfth, the same
As you exit elementary and childhood
Junior High will welcome a young lady.

Your search for identity and independence has begun
No longer can you be totally dependent on others
Take inventory and decide what you want
Charge forward to accomplish your dreams.

Be quick to listen and slow to speak
Be true to yourself and mindful of others
Set your goals high, always looking up
As you make your way to the summit.

Summertime

School is out, vacation is here
Teachers smile but parents fear
That quiet days with restful repose
Will come to an end as the school doors close.

Hungry kids who are always bored
Who clutter the house and track up the floors
No wonder mothers so often remark
I can't wait 'till fall for school to start!

Joan Pace Kennedy

To a Daughter Graduating High School

Last night, daughter, I watched
as you walked down the aisle
all dressed in shining red satin
your graduation cap and gown.

As you walked in and took your place
among the numbered class
I wondered what thoughts filled your mind.
While you sat poised and perched
on the edge of your chair
I leaned back reminiscing in mine.

Only yesterday I stood by your bed and
recalled the many times I'd kept a vigil.
But, this time was different
you weren't crying out for food or drink.
You lay there contented; you didn't need me.

Love, Laughter And Living

   Daughter, last night you left a phase
      of your life behind.
  As you exited, so did childhood.
  For now dear, you are considered
a young adult, ready to go out and face
    the traumas, trials, and troubles of the world.

Graduation erects a barrier.
   No longer can you regress and be
     totally dependent on others
    for your support and well being.
   Your search for identity and independence has begun.

  Take inventory; discover what you want in life.
  Decide the course you will pursue and charge forward
    with zest and purpose toward your goal.

Daughter, be quick to listen and
   slow to answer after deliberate thought.
   Be true to yourself and mindful of others.
   Generate happiness and remember that
    joy and peace radiate from within.

Joan Pace Kennedy

The Annual LRA State Conference

A conference, an annual state conference
The Program Chairperson, you say…
Solicit proposals and see them read
Group into grade levels and strands
Send out letters of acceptance or reject
How will I ever know what to do?

A conference, an annual state conference
How much time do I have to get it all done?
Twelve months, a whole year don't worry they say
Why that's plenty of time,
We'll help you, we'll mentor, and we'll see you through
Well then, I guess I'll just get under way.

A conference, an annual state conference
Why, there's more to this than I'd imagined
Trying to get out the Call for Proposals
For institutes, workshops, and sessions
And not wanting any to be uninformed
With the help of powers in upper circles
We got the word out… printed and on the web.

Love, Laughter And Living

A conference, an annual state conference
Why, where did the months all go
Here it is fall and the conference is at hand
We've got authors set up and exhibits to show
And there's so much still that I don't know
Like why this presenter didn't respond or confirm
Here now, let me email him again.

A conference, an annual state conference
And the Biloxi Regional comes just days before
So, amid the chaos of what we're doing
The two Chairs attend with handbills and beads
Everyone knows Louisiana is there
Beckoning attendees to come to New Orleans
For shopping, for learning, for fun.
The conference, the annual state conference
Anticipation, how the time has flown
Three full days await us, all committee planning done
Now stress and duress will see it through
The Conference Chair and Program Chair, working hand in hand, Answering questions, making decisions, and tying up loose ends
Striving to make this conference run smoothly.

The Conference, the annual LRA state conference
Near a thousand attendees, one hundred plus presenters
Even the couple of no-shows… they really didn't hinder
Volunteers at their posts, signs and A/V equipment rotating
Busy bodies moving between the three floors
There were glitches, of course, and wrinkles to smooth out
But, the gist of it was… a conference worth talking about.

The Conference, the annual LRA state conference
It has come and gone now…it is a memory

Joan Pace Kennedy

Through it all, with smiles and many well-wishes
This conference was well worth the efforts, the time
   The Conference Committee, planning sessions a plenty
   And volunteers, work and worry, and then some more
But through this united effort, together we did it,
         we made it happen.

Chapter 3
Community And Country

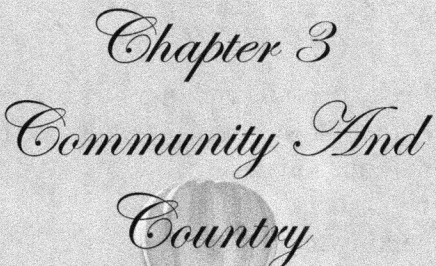

Imminent Dawn
October Madness
Laurel Hills Farm
America Stands Strong
Fallen Soldier
Land of the Free
The Guard Belongs
National Guard Duty
Gulf Shores
New England
Upper Peninsula
Hurricane Katrina
Hurricane Rita

Joan Pace Kennedy

Imminent Dawn

    Peace prevails and quietness reigns
     before the stillness is swallowed up
by muffled morning sounds -
smooth lowing of dairy cattle
    dogs barking in the distance
          and hushed strains of early risen birds.

    Not unlike the evening sounds
 of pond frogs and cadence of the locusts -
  soothing tones heard off in the darkness
      echoes of children's laughter
       waves of chatter and muffled voices
  permeate the shadowed night.

Clean morning air, fragrant with freshness
    tolerates the sounds from far away
as they drift through unobstructed airways.
Soft gentle noises, amplified
by the tranquility of the moment
    fall on the ears of the early listener.

  The pale vanishing moon continues to hover
   in the frothy, filmy, pre-dawn sky
    waiting to be chased out
    by the fierce dominance
   of the day's rising sun.

Love, Laughter And Living

Watching silently, motionless, almost reverently
feeling close to nature and in awe of the universe
cloaked in the dimness of the peaceful morning
the satisfied soul in the stillness sighs
as the body patiently waits
for the imminent dawn.

Joan Pace Kennedy

October Madness

It's time for the Fair, the hectic pace
Writing and drawing, all over the place
Children's work, done at school
Goes to the Educational Building
For visitors, by thousands, all to peruse.

On Saturday early, we move the RV
Park in an oval, friends and family we see
Spend the entire week huddled
Camped and cooking at the Fair.

Hundreds come from far and near
You never really know just who is there.
On Sunday with a shirt that declares Photography
I help receive pictures and assist in the tagging.

How do you do it, they laugh and ask
When I'm busy going and doing the tasks
Like Fair and Art and school exhibits
Working with children and their high spirits.

Love, Laughter And Living

      Story Hour, the annual Spelling Bee
      Held in the old Mt. Hermon School
           Checking to see students met the criteria
         Making sure we've all adhered to the rules.
      Long dresses and bonnets, overalls on the boys
Some wear straw hats, but we don't allow toys.

    Down by the creek, there's music and fun
      And there's Karaoke for everyone
  Who's brave enough to stand before the crowd
    And sing their song, yes…sing it out loud.

  This is part of my agenda for the month of October
It's a busy time before our break in November.
Sitting alone with my thoughts in a swirl
     Such a busy time of year for a country girl.

Joan Pace Kennedy

Laurel Hills Farm

Just two hours north of the fast lane
This Laurel Hills Farm retreat
Its cloak of wilderness
Quiet beauty and peacefulness
    Offers lush surroundings, quite unique.

None other in the parish can match it
A sense of natural environment abounds
    Undisturbed and insulated
    Fascinating showplace secluded
In the wealth of trees and foliage around.

Dogwood, pine, oak, and bay trees
Provide cover for these rolling hills
Little creatures run
Without fear of a gun
Dense underbrush, to wildlife, a refuge gives.

Winding trails through hardwood and pine
Mountain laurel and honeysuckle vine
Among budding trees or fallen leaves
    Observing animals wild and free
    Relaxing solitude, a wondrous find.

Love, Laughter And Living

  The fresh water of Crain's Creek flows gently
    Shaping the land as it follows its course
Meandering through the hollow
Such a tranquil path to follow
    Encompassed by woodland, echoing forth.

    Contentment reigns on Laurel Hills Farm
      With its horses, arena, stables, and barn
        A country home treasure
         To enjoy at leisure
      Amid the enchantment of natural charm.

Joan Pace Kennedy

America Stands Strong

Our lives were dramatically changed forever
    That fateful day, September eleven
    When our national security was stolen
    By terrorists swooping from the heavens.

Unforeseen, unexpected, and us unprepared
For such an underhanded deadly attack
Wolves in sheep's clothing entered quietly
    And masterfully "stabbed" us in the back.

They took advantage of USA generosity
    And our open-door policy was swell
    For groups to come get a fine education
    Some trained to become pilots as well.

Then using their knowledge and expertise
For that deadly destructive adventure
Hijacked two planes and brought them down
    Bombing the World Trade Center.

The twin towers fell and still another plane
    Was headed for our national spire
But this one fell short and missed its mark
Yet the Pentagon was heavily damaged by fire.

Love, Laughter And Living

We no longer feel safe, but ill at ease
Suspicious and wary, not secure anymore
Our trust and our faith have been shaken
And we're injured to the very core.

But we'll recover and be stronger for it
No terrorist strike will victory win
For the USA stands united and firm
And the bell of freedom still rings.

Patriotism is very much alive
Its blood flows through our veins
And through the turmoil and the strife
We'll bind up our wounds, endure the pain.

For our country is more than tall buildings
We're friends and neighbors, heart and soul strong
And our millions who make up this body
Keep America energized and going on and on.

Fallen Soldier

One of our own has fallen, a soldier
On the battlefield fighting for right.
Blood spilled on the ground in a foreign land
In the midst of an Afghanistan fight.

The bullets were flying and one reached its mark
Deep behind his vest, tearing through his chest and beyond
He fell to the ground, not quite comprehending
As a medical officer rushed to do his best.

Under a steady barrage of live enemy fire
This dedicated medic never left his side
Applying pressure precise, he stopped the abdomen flow
Saving the soldier's life, we know.

Heroic measures followed, from the battlefield they fled
To the nearest facility; then, surgery to save his life.
More blood loss and corrective operations followed from
Ghazni to Bagram to Germany, where they finally arrived.

In fear, in shock…a continent away, in the USA
Family members and friends gathered to pray.
Reaching out to give comfort to one another
By word or deed, or cooking to feed.

Love, Laughter And Living

With updates given to the family in wait
Each day, not knowing, was pure torment.
Then the caseworker negotiated the awaited phone call
And the son garbled his words to a happy mom and dad.

In time, the progress report was impressive
With news that he'd soon be coming home...
Home, that is, to an American hospital
Where back in his homeland, in time he will heal.

Give God the glory for this life that was saved
    He's been saved twice now and he knows it.
He'll have a personal testimony with others to share
        As he tells of the miracles of the great Physician.
           He served his country with honor and pride
His Bible and prayer gave him guidance and strength.
        Through the mercy of God, this soldier was spared
To return home, knowing he's done his patriotic duty.

Joan Pace Kennedy

Land of the Free

This world is full of wondrous folds
Outstanding beauties to behold
The sun, the moon, and stars so bright
Comets and asteroids in the night
Other planets out of sight
Make up our universe so bold.

Bountiful grass so rich and green
Blankets of flowers to be seen
Birds with nests up in the trees
Busy hives filled with bees
Swarming in the summer breeze
Creating an atmosphere serene.

Stately trees rise to the sky
Their arms outstretched, unfurled
With trunks and limbs of brown
Roots penetrating the ground
They're so nice to have around
Wherever you are in the world.

Love, Laughter And Living

        Galaxies full of stars so bright
     Out in the dark beyond
Flickering slightly
      Glittering brightly
          Sought our nightly
       Of these we've grown quite fond.

        Across the barren desert
         Over the fruitful plain
Up mountain peaks
In quiet, cool creeks
          Its solitude he seeks
       As he listens to nature's refrain.

     How long since he's seen a river flow
       Or watched the sun as it set low
         Too busy with life
         Children and wife
        Encumbered with strife
            Too often, he's just on the go.

     America, land of opportunity
But how many take time to see
The rocks, trees, and flowers
        Bubbling brooks that are ours
              To enjoy endless hours
          All in this land of the free.

Joan Pace Kennedy

The Guard Belongs

The National Guard has long been known
    As one who lends a hand
In time of strife or trouble
        Throughout our country's land.

    Off they're sent to guard and protect
    Where civilian men aren't allowed
        Stand watch over businesses in a flood
    Control a riot or calm a crowd.

    When N.O.P.D. went out on strike
        The Guard was called to duty
        For Mardi Gras, it had to go on
    Tradition, throws, and beauty.

    In flood, famine, and earthquake disasters
The Guard is always there
    In time of need, they show the world
    There is someone to care.

    It's not always easy for the men to leave
    Their families for training camp
        To go on maneuvers or mile long hikes
Sleep in the woods, often cold and damp.

Love, Laughter And Living

They train to be ready to meet the need
Of whatever task they face
    Some become leaders, outstanding in rank
    Still others go at their own pace.

The Guard belongs, they do their share
    To help our country grow
        Community, school, and city projects
    The Guard is ready, on the go.

Down to Panama in Central America
    Is the latest move they've made
In lieu of their summer camp, the men
    Down there for two weeks have stayed.

To a far out village, somewhat remote
    Their task has been building a road
        The poor people there respect and admire
    These men who have shouldered the load.

Camp Gato Solo is their base
Tent City, it's sometimes called
Sleeping on cots, living out of their bags
    The same is for one and all.

An experience that all will remember
    This trip to that south central land
        It was yet another good-will venture
    For the U.S. and National Guard man.

Joan Pace Kennedy

National Guard Duty

If we must part and you must go
    Away for just a while
My love will follow you my dear
        To warm you across the miles.

For where you are, there I am too
    Though only in your mind
        My heart is with you darling
    A love more true, you'll never find.

My thoughts are with you daily
    I dream of you each night
        I long to take you in my arms
Want you to hold me tight.

I know there's work that must be done
    And you want to do your part
        So I will wait and keep your love
    Alive here in my heart.

I'm proud of you, that you would go
    To serve your country well
As a Guardsman, as a Minuteman
    Do whatever the job entails.

But now I'm ready for your return
I'm tired of being left alone
I want you here at home with family
And from Panama, "Be Gone!"

Joan Pace Kennedy

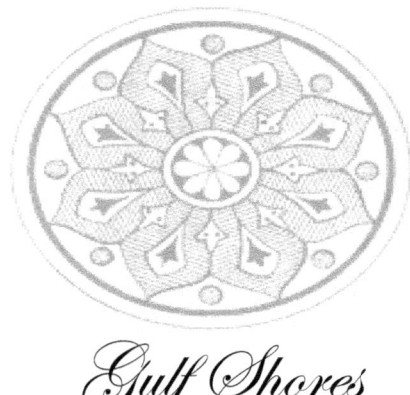

Gulf Shores

Bright water rushed to meet us
Throwing up waves of welcome
Hearty heaves of excitement.

White caps nibbling sandy beach
Wearing a wide open grin
Gleamed in glaring summer sun.

Breakers gracefully performing
Suddenly erupted in frolic
Then hurried to greet the shore.

Rolling, salty billows rose
Rushed to reach the silent sand
Forcing a fleeting encounter.

A washboard of delicate ripples
Imprinted by the washing waves
Left a message soon erased.

New England

New Hampshire, known as the Granite State
Rightfully so, make no mistake
Mountains, boulders, and rocks abound
Strewn over fields, the woods, and grounds.

A part of New England, it stands apart
As an early colony at America's start
Full of mystique and natural beauty
Folks live and breathe their patriotic duty.

License plates proclaim, "Live free or die"
Residents proudly hang flags to fly
Always in a hurry, rushing to and fro
Locals and visitors with places to go.

So much to see where our history began
The Atlantic waves roll on beaches of sand
On rocky boulders, they beat with a fist
Crashing the sea walls, spraying fine mist.

Lighthouses of Maine, their foghorns clear
A message for ships and vessels to hear
Guiding and warning of dangers lurking
To ensure safe harbor, the keeper is working.

Joan Pace Kennedy

New Hampshire is truly a vacationer's dream
From the ocean, to mountains, to backwoods streams
Both rich in history and old from birth
A most picturesque corner of God's green earth.

Love, Laughter And Living

Upper Peninsula

On the shores of Gitche Gumee
Way up north from Louisian
He went there to lay a pipeline
While she just followed that man.

Another state to add to others
Amassing over the years
Beginning in sixty-seven
Concluding with who knows when.

So many sights and wonders
New places to explore
In the northern state of Michigan
On the Gitche Gumee shore.

Rich timber, pelts, and iron ore
Explorers learned their worth
Lush country, north, the Upper P
Resources like none other on earth.

They cut down trees, trapped for furs
Ravaged and raped the land
They mined rich ore, settled the towns
Erected saunas and houses to stand.

Joan Pace Kennedy

Against the winters and bitter cold
They braved and forged ahead
To leave their mark in history
And today it can be said…

That the people who settled the northern U.P.
Were a hearty and fearless band
Migrating in search of a better life
And settling on Superior land.

Love, Laughter And Living

Hurricane Katrina

For days we knew she was coming
TV and Radio blared it out on all sides
This category five storm, she's a big one
With waves more than forty feet high.

The winds were a force with which to reckon
They tore down anything in or near their path
Tornados spawned and the roar was distinguished
Above the slamming, tearing, and rain's downpour.

Mighty oaks and huge pine trees were uprooted
Stands of trees were snapped off like matchsticks
Rooftops were gone and the rain poured in
Residents left homeless, without much of their own.

The rush of the wind cleared a path as it moved
Over land and sea, leaving havoc behind
Bridges washed out and boats were thrown inland
Debris hurled around and strewn out over miles.

The swift, swirling water rose higher and higher
Invading, eroding both highways and homes
Forcefully flooding and menacingly destroying
Filling a bowl until it was overflowing.

Joan Pace Kennedy

    Disbelief, disheartened, and displaced
  Mandatory evacuations left many in shelters
        Some folks left early in their efforts to escape
Other residents traveled slowly for many long miles.

    Some of the warnings just were not heeded
    Others listened, but waited too late to leave
        Many of those who adamantly refused
  Suffered as they waited to be rescued.

  Then there were those who were stranded
  Those who sat on their rooftops for days
      But they fared better than those afloat or aside
The ones who didn't make it out alive.

  A hurricane is not to be taken lightly
  The strength of tornado winds will displace
  We must evacuate whenever necessary
Or take shelter in a far away safe place.

    Katrina has definitely earned a place in our history
Exceeding the notorious Betsy and Camille
    Not only with the massive damages incurred
        But in the breadth of her destruction's field.

  Strong forces of nature, man cannot control
  We're humbled as we watch her perform
And reminded that in a contest between man and nature
  Those awesome forces of Nature will always win.

  Through it all, we came through with thanksgiving
    For the realization of what could have been
So, we're giving thanks for the things that were spared
And trying not to dwell on things gone and destroyed.

Love, Laughter And Living

Hurricane Rita

To feel so helpless as you listen to every word
Newscasters reporting and it's not good news we've heard
Out in the Gulf, there's another storm turning
And our hearts and emotions and fears are all churning.

This other storm is brewing and of this we've never heard
Two back to back
with over a hundred sixty mile an hour winds
Hurricane Katrina, so destructive while alive
Now Hurricane Rita's in the
Gulf and she's a Category Five.

The southeast coast was wiped out and flooded
For a span of more than two hundred miles
Now our cautious neighbors to the west
Are diligently looking for somewhere safe to hide.

Never in the history of our country are we told
Of two Fives being recorded in the same hurricane season
But, here within weeks is another slamming force
That's headed for Texas and a four hundred mile coast.

Joan Pace Kennedy

Forces of Nature, we have no reign to pull back
No way to avoid them, just prepare in their track
Evacuate, get ready, don't tempt fate with your life
  Structures can be rebuilt, but you can't resurrect lives lost.

Chapter 4
Faith And Friends

Faith is the Key
Thankfulness
He's Always There
You Never Left Me
Our Faith
Travel by Faith
Well Done?
The Parson on a Sunday Morn
God is Alive
Why Did You Come?
Get to Know the Lord
Christians
Missy, the Missionary
Heaven
My Prayer
Close to Thee
Blessed Assurance
Don't Give Up
Chances Are
Call to Service
Jesus, the Savior
He's the One
No Better Friend
Friendship
Reflections at Day's End

Joan Pace Kennedy

Faith is the Key

Faith is the substance of things hoped for
    A belief without ever a question
            The evidence of things not seen
    A trust needing no verification.

    By faith Abraham offered Isaac, his son
But the angel stayed his hand
And it was faith that brought the children out
    Of the wilderness to the promise land.

Oh great the faith of those three Hebrew men
        Who were cast into the furnace of fire
      Yet God walked there in the midst of them
For they obeyed His will and desire.

It was truly by faith that Noah stepped out
      Building the ark of old
He simply took the Lord at His word
      And did as he was told.

Because of that faith, his family and he
Were saved when the rains came down
Flooding the earth, destroying the land
Leaving neither city nor town.

David through faith defied the giant
On the battlefield that day
This young shepherd boy with only a sling
Had a God who directed his way.

Faith is that guiding hand that leads
Directing our pathway, our journey, our flight
Through faith we are able to take a stand
For faith in God adds dimension to life.

Only through faith can we arise
Go out and face each day
For faith is the key that unlocks the door
Then God will lead the way.

Joan Pace Kennedy

Thankfulness

As each new day begins to dawn
As sunlight breaks the sky
I close my eyes in silent prayer
So thankful Lord am I.

For all your many blessings, God
For happiness, peace, and joy
For home and family, lots of friends
My husband, girls, and boy.

Lest I forget whose hand it is
That holds my life intact
Lord make me ever mindful
Of the way I talk and act.

Help me to strive to live upright
That my life be not in vain
And seek to share with others
The glory of Thy name.

He's Always There

Is your life like a roller-coaster
With emotional lows and highs?
Peaks of exhilaration don't last long enough
Then into valleys of depression you slide.

Emotions can become overwhelming.
Even Christians are not immune.
But if we cast all our care upon Him
He'll relieve the tension because He cares.

The key to a stable emotional life
Is learning how to handle our feelings
Recognizing the problems and critical areas
Trusting Him always to lift life's heavy burdens.

Difficult times come to everyone
Not a soul is left unscathed.
But sharing our troubles with the blessed Lord
Will deepen our faith, giving us strength and comfort.

It's a privilege to be able to call on God
Assured that He'll always be there.
He knows our every need before we ask
Sees our weakness and invites us to lean on Him.

Joan Pace Kennedy

Problems, of course, will often occur.
We weren't promised a life without stress.
Yet the One powerful enough to guide all creation
Is still willing to love and care for us.

Love, Laughter And Living

You Never Left Me

You ferried me over the troubled waters
Through the sorrows and the grief
And Lord, You never left me.

You guided me when I had no direction
Took my burden and gave relief
Yea Lord, You never left me.

You carried me when I was weak and weary
No strength to carry on my belief
Yet Lord, You never left me.

You cared even when I was rebellious
Rebuked and chastened my conceit
But Lord, you never left me.

Your promise You have truly kept
To never leave me nor forsake
Yes Lord, I know, You never left me.

Joan Pace Kennedy

Our Faith

Faith is the substance of things unseen
Belief in a heaven that we can't yet visit
Dependence on a Savior in whom we've trusted
    To take us to a place we only have heard of.

Faith is the evidence of things not seen
    A language we use without audible sounds
Unsaid words only the Lord understands
He gives us comfort and peace unexplainable.

It's only through Faith that we can survive
Trials, tragedies, and sufferings of life
    The many obstacles encountered each day
In our struggle to live for God and do His will.

Clinging to our Faith, we hold on
    To our trust and belief in the Almighty
Knowing that when the end shall come
He will deliver and we will forever reign with Him.

Love, Laughter And Living

Travel by Faith

Life is a continuous journey
    That every one of us takes
   And the many roads that we travel
Lead to golden opportunity breaks.

  Up one hill and down another
Around a bend in the road
  Down vast stretches of scenic views
    Past where the highway bows.

  Then up crops unexpected obstacles
That slow the daily pace
  They change the very facet of life
    And put us in our place.

  Who knows what early morn will bring
    When we retire at night
  Our travel plans may be revamped
    At the dawning of daylight.

  So let us live that if and when
    We're dealt a brand new hand
  That's oh so different from the one
    We had so carefully planned.

Joan Pace Kennedy

We're able to swerve, not overcorrect
And soon be back in the race
To continue our journey, absorbing the bumps
And happily travel with joy and faith.

Love, Laughter And Living

Well Done?

Moments spent together
The time we have on earth
Seasons we shared
The lives we lived
Remain in memory
To be recalled with pleasure
With sadness or satisfaction
In days to come.

Touched by someone
Taught by many
Influenced by a multitude
Impressed by a few
Moved by the crowd
Compelled by the legions
Inspired from above.

Life lived to the fullest
Living, loving, learning
Giving and sharing
Doing what's needed
Then life is over

Joan Pace Kennedy

Death comes to all
And we face our Maker.
What will He say?

Love, Laughter And Living

The Parson on a Sunday Morn

In solemn silence he stood
Staring out at the congregation
Knowing eyes sweeping the pews
Acknowledging those present,
Mentally tallying the absent.

His gaze slowly wandered
Encompassed the waiting audience
Peered at the empty seats
The vacant spaces, unoccupied benches
Witnessing against their missing members.

He stood there in the pulpit alone
Just one before the crowd
As the One who had come before him
And humbly bowed his head…

Lord, thank you for this Lord's Day
And those gathered here to pray.

God is Alive

God is alive, He's on His throne
Watching over His children below
    He sits and muses over sinful men
Considers how far He'll let them go.

Wicked cities, unrighteous towns
Populations without care for the Lord
    God sends His message loud and clear
Through chosen men who minister His word.

Like prophets of old, they travel about
    As missionaries far and wide
        So hard to leave their home and family
But God promised to be by their side.

    God is alive, He is not dead!
        Just witness His vast creation
            I know He died and rose again
To provide a plan of salvation.

    God is alive, I'm glad He lives
        Always and evermore
            Because He lives, my soul is saved
Blessed Savior, my Jesus, my Lord!

Love, Laughter And Living

Why Did You Come?

For what reason did you come
Asked the man of God out loud
Did you come to seek a blessing
Or just be one of the crowd?

Was the weather picture perfect
So you ventured here today?
Why did you come to service?
I heard the preacher say.

Was it for some earthly reason
That you sought the house of God?
Or were you hungry for the word
And so our path you trod?

Were you searching for that inner peace,
That passes understanding?
The kind that only comes from God
The one that's everlasting.

Why did you come to church today?
Was it only to be seen?
Or did you come to praise the Lord
To worship and to sing?

Joan Pace Kennedy

God knows your heart and soul, my friend
He's watching from above.
Did you come to church to know Him
To experience His love?

No matter what the reason was
    That brought you out this way
    God's grace is all sufficient
Won't you be saved today?

Then, when the preacher asks you
Why is it that you've come?
    You'll answer with a happy smile
To exalt God's precious Son!

Love, Laughter And Living

Get to Know the Lord

Do you really know the Lord
    Or do you just know about Him?
        Can you talk to the Holy God
Or can you only talk about Him?

    His unconditional love is real
Know Him, know He's there.
    For all times, His promise is real
        His grace and comfort to share.

      Praise Him in the good times
      In the happy times and sad
      Call on Him and give thanks
        Be thankful for His many blessings.

Don't wait until some tragedy
    Brings you to your knees
        To call on Him, in your darkness
For His mercy in time of need.

Christians

Sunday morning meeting times
Churches, Christ, and Christians
Buildings, benches, beat-up bars
Where many stood and prayed their prayers.

Sanctuaries, songs, and service
Passionate pastors preaching
Friends and family, favorite hymns
Faith and freedom from sins forgiven.

Believe, be saved, and then baptized
Begin to follow Him
Trying to be like the Father
Temptations and trials are sure to follow.

Bible teachings, biblical truths
Outline the manner and show the way
As a congregation gathers
To raise their voices in praise.

Books and verses, stories told
Passages, parables, from days of old
Mirror and measure, gauge and judge
As we hear the word and message bold.

Love, Laughter And Living

Sunday morning meeting times
Midweek service too
Walking each day with our Savior and Lord
Seeking the things He wants us to do.

Joan Pace Kennedy

Missy, the Missionary

Madam, they call the lady
The one who spreads the word
    The gospel of God's precious Son
        To those who have not heard.

A lily amid the darkness
Of skin and understanding
    But when Jesus opens up the heart
The light shines from within.

New life creates new creatures
    The old man's cast aside
        The wonder of being a Christian
Amazes the native child.

For we are all babes in Christ
When first we're born again
    But through the word of God we grow
By giving our life to Him.

Contented to serve and follow the Lord
    Over land and waters wide
        Takes a special person with love and faith
And God-given grace and style.

Heaven

Heaven's not so far away
    Traveling won't take long
    When Jesus gives the final call
I'll make my journey home.

Right through the clouds, I'll make my climb
    Up to the judgment hall
This trip is one that all must take
    When comes the Master's call.

    There my Savior will be waiting
        Welcome home, I'll hear Him say
        And I'll praise the name of Jesus
    Who washed my sins away.

Oh, how happy will be that greeting
        When I meet Him face to face
    The one who loved me dearly
Enough to die, He took my place.

Now forever I'll adore Him
As I worship around the throne
And give thanks to God in heaven
For His Son and my heavenly home.

Joan Pace Kennedy

My Prayer

Let not my prayers be selfish
But for a higher motive strive
      To grow in grace and knowledge
Of my saving Jesus Christ.

Lord, give me strength to stand for Thee
To ever humbly seek Thy face
      And not forget that sinners like me
Were saved by Your marvelous grace.

Not for my own personal comfort
Nor material wealth or gain
      Lord, let my prayers be selfless
Whenever I call on Thy name.

Your son was sent to ransom me
To rescue from sin and give new life
      Placed the love of Christ down deep within
And gives peace in the midst of daily strife.

Close to Thee

Lord guide me in the right direction
My life is filled with imperfection.

The devil attacks from every side
It seems there is no place to hide.

Shield me, Jesus, hold me strong
Forgive me when my way is wrong.

Strengthen my faith, help me through
Grant that I serve and follow You.

Open my eyes to Satan's wiles
Remember God, I am your child.

Nurture me Lord that I might grow
And seeds of Christian charity sow.

My heart's desire and prayer will be
That you always keep me close to Thee.

Joan Pace Kennedy

Blessed Assurance

You ask me why I'm optimistic
Why I feel everything will be all right.
When you turn the problem over to the Lord
He'll guide through each dark and lonely night.

When we stood by the bed of our daughter
In the hospital so big and impersonal
Knowing full well that she might not live
God in his mercy watched over us there.

Then we laid our little son to rest
In the grave beneath the sod
Just the week before Thanksgiving
Amid the tears, we counted our blessings.

Even when pneumonia struck me down
And I was hovering at death's door
God never left my bedside and He
Blessed me to recover, renewed my strength once more.

Why shouldn't I be optimistic?
Who could ask for anything more?
We have our health and our family
And this is wealth, in a sense, immeasurable.

Love, Laughter And Living

Blessings have been bestowed on us
By our Father, God in heaven above.

Joan Pace Kennedy

Don't Give Up

Don't give up,
Get down on your knees.
When the going gets rough
Just ask the Lord please
To answer your prayer
If it be His will.
Brother don't give up,
Get down on your knees.

He's waited so long
Just to hear from you.
But don't worry my friend
He'll see you through
This trouble and strife
Though your faith may be weak.
Don't give up my friend,
Get down on your knees.

When God looks down
From heaven above
And shares with us
His matchless love

Love, Laughter And Living

He'll cure your ills
    of sin and disease.
Brother don't give up,
Get down on your knees.

Joan Pace Kennedy

Chances Are...

Chances are we'll meet again
If not in this life
Then at the end.

Chances are with saints of old
We'll stroll on streets
All paved with gold.

Chances are the heavens will ring
With joyous praise
Glad songs we'll sing.

Chances are our souls will rejoice
For long ago
We made Jesus our choice.

But, chances are only chances
And our lives are so uncertain
So make sure of your salvation
Before the closing of death's curtain.

Call to Service

The fields are white to harvest
   The laborers are so few
        We should be ever mindful
  Of winning souls for You.

Seldom do we venture forth
   To share the gospel word
        With unsuspecting fellow men
Who have never of You heard.

Surely there's a work to do
   If only we would heed
        The call to be of service
  As on Your word we feed.

Step boldly out into the world
   Proclaim the message clear
      Spreading the news of a Savior's love
  To everyone who will hear.

Joan Pace Kennedy

Jesus, the Savior

Souls adrift on the sea of life
Sin and strife have blinded their eyes
Not even knowing they need a rescue
Then through God's word
They learn of Your compassionate love!

Lost souls drifting, about to sink
Perhaps today, just one
On the brink of accepting
Salvation's message,
The glad, glad news.

He listens,
He learns,
He truly believes
Oh, dear Jesus,
A precious soul receives!

One less to burn in a fiery hell
Praise the Lord, the preacher's message did tell
Of Jesus' death on the cruel cross
Raised from the dead, He paid the cost
Now, because He lives, a soul's not lost.

He's the One

The earth was all dark, black as in night
Until Jesus said, "Let there be light."
The world was wicked, full of sin and strife
Then Jesus came, on the cross gave His life.

My steps were faltering, the way rough and long
Then Jesus called saying, "Child I'll make you strong."
If your life is troubled, you feel weak and undone
Remember now the Savior, for He is the One.

The One who created the earth and blue sky
Prepared for those who trust Him, a mansion up on high.
The One who left Heaven to save us from sin
Made a way of salvation for all wayward men.

The One who is there to hear our petitions
To shower us with love and multitudes of blessings.
He is the One, the only One, glorious in grace is He
In childlike faith accept Him and forever you will be free.

Joan Pace Kennedy

No Better Friend

When on life's sea of struggle
Of hustle, bustle, and stress
When problems seem to overtake
And put you to the test.

Remember there is someone
Who wants to share your load
He'll guide, guard, and direct you
As you travel on life's road.

He'll be your friend in trouble
He'll help you through your strife
And be right there to comfort you
Through the dark and lonely night.

No better friend is Jesus
Who gave his life for you
Won't you give your heart to Him
Begin your life anew?

Friendship

    Friendship is a kind of tie
                That bonds one to another
            A friend is one who'll stick to you
                As close as your own brother
    Through thick and thin,
To the journey's end,
He'll be there like no other.

      In friendship there is never room
          For jealousy and strife
              Friends you make in early years
                  Can last throughout your life
        A comrade kind,
       Help in a bind,
   An ally any time of night.

Joan Pace Kennedy

Reflection at Day's End

Did you help the poor and needy
Or shoulder someone's load?
Did you share a bit of happiness
With the travelers on life's road?

    Did you join the others with head held high
    To lift your voice in praise
    To the One who's blessed you all the while
    Cared for you through your days?

    Did you offer a prayer of thanksgiving
For family, home and friends
And thank the Lord for heaven above
    That waits at our journey's end?

Whenever you pause to reflect on your life
    Is it all you would like it to be?
Is the picture there, one of which you are proud
    For others to stop, view, and see?

    Did you give of yourself to others
    The lonely, the sick, or the blind?
It's not always money these folks may need
    Sometimes they'd just like your time.

Love, Laughter And Living

Take time to talk and listen
To those who are down in despair.
It requires so very little of you
Yet it lets them know you care.

It may be a humble deed
A smile or simply a word.
But you might lift the spirits
Of the many who go unheard.

So make your life richer, sweeter by far
As you strive toward your goals.
Give of yourself, throw out a lifeline
On which someone just might take a hold.

Joan Pace Kennedy

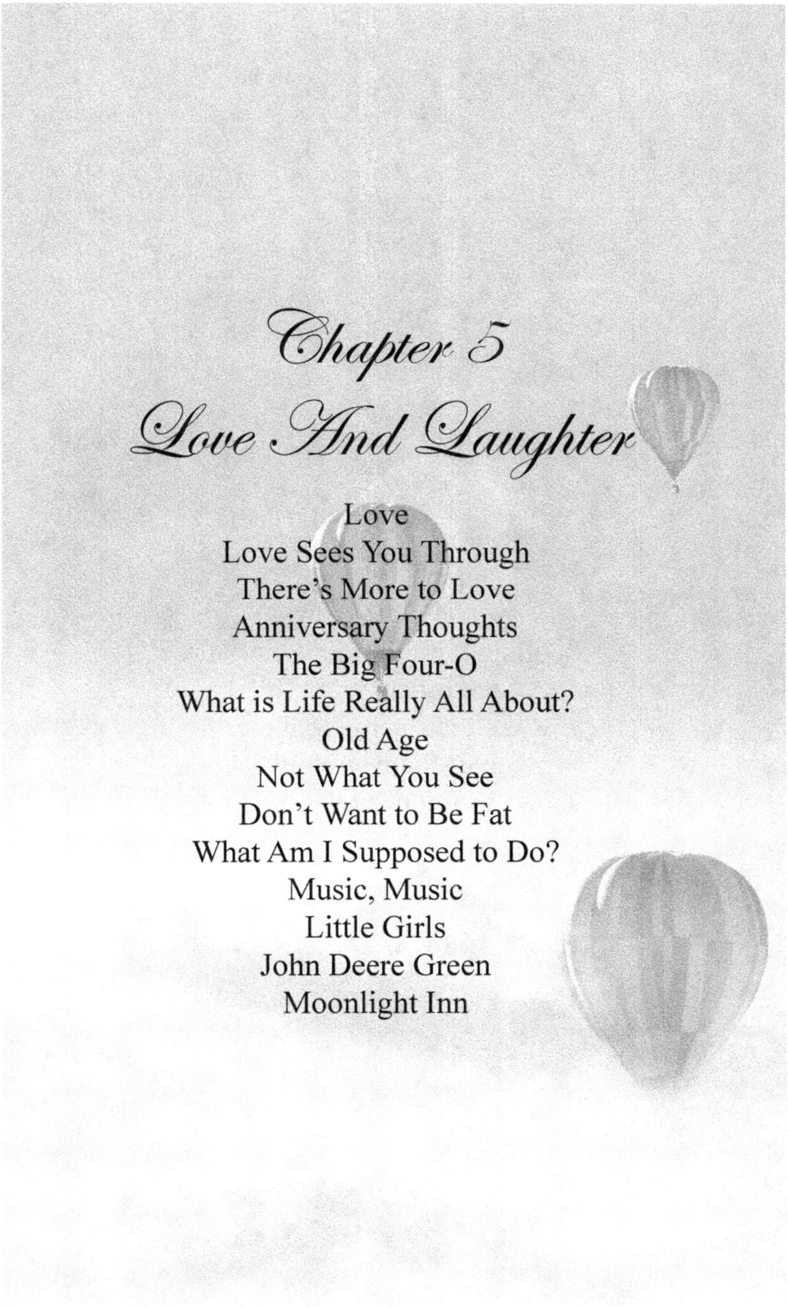

Chapter 5
Love And Laughter

Love
Love Sees You Through
There's More to Love
Anniversary Thoughts
The Big Four-O
What is Life Really All About?
Old Age
Not What You See
Don't Want to Be Fat
What Am I Supposed to Do?
Music, Music
Little Girls
John Deere Green
Moonlight Inn

Joan Pace Kennedy

Love

A man
and a woman
coping with the challenges
of the modern day life
where their being together
gives them strength
and needed
courage.

Love, Laughter And Living

Love Sees You Through

Once you've had love, it never really goes away.
Although our parents have moved to another "room",
They're still in our hearts, our minds,
and our homes every day.
Love keeps them alive and gives us a warm, secure feeling.

That love sees us through the pain, the loss, the void
As we lean on each other, remembering the good times
Recalling with familiarity scenes
and stories from childhood
Looking to and asking God for strength and comfort.

Love is that warm, fuzzy blanket that envelopes us
Memories are the kindling for the fires that burn
Keeping our precious loved ones with us
Long after they're gone from our presence here.

Joan Pace Kennedy

There's More to Love

There is more to love than candy
Than flowers, wine, and cards
There is something to be said for
The man who is working hard.

The man who is steady, always there
Ready to lend a hand
The man who says, "I like you!"
To a wife who understands.

There is more to love than verbal woos
Than compliments galore
He told her once he loved her
Years back-more than three score.

No reason to repeat it daily
Why should he say it all the time
He said he loved her years ago
He hasn't changed his mind.

Sure of himself and of her too
Romance is just a word
He is sure she knows what is in his heart
Though not from what she has heard.

Love, Laughter And Living

    Secure in knowing he is there for her
                      Regardless of what befalls
                    He travels far away on jobs
  She is there with just one call.

    He calls to say I need you
                      I want you here with me
  And off she flies wherever
  That man of hers might be.

Joan Pace Kennedy

Anniversary Thoughts

Soft words and mellow music
    Written by the waves
           Recorded on the sand
        Too soon they're washed away.

For the rhythm of the lapping
    The shallow waters wait
           Waves inhale as in they roll
           Exhale as out they fade.

The steady ebb, the gentle flow
    The chronic cycle of the sea
           Smooth patterns of the universe
    Resemble you and me.

Love, Laughter And Living

The Big Four- O

I always thought being forty was old
        Until by birthday came this year
          It's not at all like I expected
    And certainly not what I had feared.

As a child the idea of forty years old
    Seemed elderly and ancient to me
        But I had no real concept of time
    And thought growing up would take an eternity.

I entered my teens and mother turned forty
    Of course, I considered that aged
For she was mom and I was a teenager
    How could she possibly not be old?

    Then I became a wife and mother
    And my opinions changed dramatically
        It was now to mom I frequently turned
    For her youthful advice and counsel.

Well here I am forty – I have arrived
    The journey was brief, believe me
But age has not hampered my feelings inside
    The big "four-o" has not made me old.

Joan Pace Kennedy

Now that forty is young, fifty's not old
Nor sixty or even sixty-five
And with a little luck I'll be able to say
I feel young, as long as I'm alive.

What Is Life Really All About?

Supper is done, the dishes await
As I sit in my rocker and contemplate
    Life and its mysteries, days gone by
And think how swiftly time does fly.

Was it only yesterday with babies small
The floor was cluttered wall to wall
    Now here I sit and rock alone
Kids grown up and far from home.

The years were filled with laughter and fun
And a lot of pain caused tears to run
    But that blanket of love was always there
Like church and music, a song and a prayer.

Many a day was spent rushing around
Off to work, to school, to town
    College classes – a higher degree
Jobs and travel for him and me.

Joan Pace Kennedy

The first half of life is gone – youth is spent
    Sitting here wondering now where it went
It is time to slow down as the years run out
    Is this what life is really about?

Old Age

Who is that in the mirror, I half-heard myself say
Why, I didn't look that old, when I looked yesterday.

Old age has crept in like a fog on the woods
And we find that old body no longer works as it should.

Our youth is used up on folly and gone…
Now we're left with aches and creaks in our bones.

But that fog rolls on in like the sea to the shore
Can't shut it out with brick walls or thick doors.

That unwelcome stranger takes a prominent seat
And affects what we see, how we hear, what we eat.

Rudely, without asking, he takes away one by one
Our entire independence and power to run.

We then come full circle from the day of our birth
To the end of our time and life here on earth.

Old age comes to all, if you're blessed, you'll agree
Because many die young and old age never see.

Joan Pace Kennedy

Not What You See

Oh dear me, it's already evening
The sun's sinking low in the west
I pause for a moment to glance 'round me
And try to see what I've done today.

Piles of dirty dishes are washed and stored
The kitchen linoleum is mopped
The cabinets and shelves are dusted
But, can you see anything I've done?

The washer and dryer have been busy
Clean clothes are folded and put away
But just by looking about here
Can you see what I've done today?

Coats are hung and the boots put away
Playthings in the toy box for a while will stay
Not an idle minute have I had all day
But what have I done that you see?

The beds are made and floors are swept
The carpet has been vacuumed again
    Bathrooms are clean and the air smells sweet
Yet what I've done, can anyone see?

For after working all day on everyday chores
        It is not what I have done that you see
The only way you would really take notice
Is if those tasks were left UNDONE by me.

Don't Want to Be Fat

Fat though I am, I don't plan to be
Obese, rotund, or pleasantly padded
      That reflection is not my new intention
From now on you'll see some will power added.

My purpose is simple, it's painfully clear
Less food, lower calories, more exercise
      Beginning today, I'll watch what I eat
Smaller portions will help, I've just realized.

Such a strict undertaking is nothing new
I've begun this journey before
      Somehow I never reach my destination
Which necessitates the same trip over and over.

A child can be chubby, an old lady stout
But me, in the middle, I just want OUT!
      Don't want to be big, spilling out of my dress,
Rolls of fat bulging from under my breast.

A corpulent figure is surely not my intent
I want excess weight gone, to be really content
      But like so many others, I just love to eat
And to lose a few pounds is a feat...repeat!

Love, Laughter And Living

What Am I Supposed to Do?

You told me you loved me a long time ago
    On the day when we both said, I do.
Now you say you don't love me anymore
    So, what am I supposed to do?

I can't stop the sun, can't turn off the rain
So, how can you expect me to live with the pain
    Of letting you go to find somebody new
    Oh, what am I supposed to do?

You made me your wife when we first spoke those vows
    You promised to love me forever
    Now you're trying to say that it's no longer true
    Just what am I supposed to do?

I can't turn off the rain, can't block out the sun
I don't want to go looking for a new someone
    It seems you've already made up your mind
    But, what am I supposed to do?

Such terrible, hurtful words have been said
The scenes are still playing out in my head
My heart's full of sorrow and bitter tears
    Now, what am I supposed to do?

Joan Pace Kennedy

Music, Music

Music, a song…a note, a phrase
Touches our hearts in so many ways
Uptown beat, the lowdown words
Mournful sounds for years we've heard.

Soothing strains of a melody
Simple, pure, and sweet
Drift across and through the mind
To some we smile, to others we weep.

But, nothing ever stirs the soul
Or reaches quite so deep
As a heart-wrenching tune
Or a boot-scootin' beat.

Centuries old, traditional songs
Hymnal words, etched in stone
Wondrous stories set to music
Their gifted artists, now long gone.

Rhythm and rhyme never die
Lyrics written here and there
Live on in our minds, our hearts
Words on our lips, and in the air.

Little Girls

Little girls are heaven sent
To change the course of man
The long fine hair
And skin so fair
Tempts you to hold her hand.

The blushing girl with eyes of blue
Bashful, shy, and coy
She'll do her part
To win your heart
If you're the lucky boy.

For there she waits in all her beauty
Without conceit or pretentious air
Demure and shy
As men pass by
Will you let her know you care?

Should you decide she is the one
With whom you'll spend your life
Confess your love
Beneath stars above
Ask her to be your wife.

Joan Pace Kennedy

Then down life's road you'll travel
Together hand in hand
Little blue-eyed girl
Who was daddy's world
Has changed the course of this one man.

Love, Laughter And Living

John Deere Green

My favorite color is John Deere green
Around our house, that's all that's seen.

Mowing the grass with a John Deere mower
Cleaning the leaves with the John Deere blower.

Cutting firewood with a saw of John Deere
Keeps the family warm year after year.

With a JD weed-eater, trimming's not such a chore
The John Deere generator goes camping by the shore.

That old two-cylinder with its putt-putt sound
Pulled a lot of plows to cultivate our ground.

There's a 650 dozer of John Deere yellow
And the owner knows he's a lucky fellow

That a man long ago by the name of John Deere
Designed hardy equipment that lasts many long years.

Joan Pace Kennedy

Moonlight Inn

Nestled in the crook of the river and the road
The Moonlight Inn shines oh, so bright
Crowds mill around and the drinks flow steady
For men who come in and those who are ready.

In bayou country where slow waters abound
Land lies low and lots of seafood is found
Many a good times had, with family and friends
As the music plays loud at the Moonlight Inn.

There is always a party at the river's bend
Don't miss the fun at this Moonlight Inn
For a place to stop off and unload your care
With a round of drinks or just a bottle of beer.

The outside's not fancy, not dressed up at all
But you'll know that you're welcome, because
You'll hear someone call, y'all come on in
Make yourself at home, here at Moonlight Inn.

No dress code necessary, no long waiting line
Doors always spring open and the service is fine
So when you're down south, near the river's bend
Pass yourself a good time at the Moonlight Inn.
Folks come and go; but they always leave with a grin
After their "good time" visit to the Moonlight Inn.

Love, Laughter And Living

Chapter 6
Holidays And Happiness

To Everything, There is a Season
The Emergence of Spring
Spring
Golden Autumn
Father's Day Tribute
What is Happiness?
Finally Friday
Clouds Like…
Relaxation
Rain
Raindrops
Summer Showers
Rainbow of Colors
Nature's Palette
Optimism
The Sun
Sunshine
Day vs. Night
Christmas

Joan Pace Kennedy

To Everything, There is a Season

During the course of time and
Across the span of life
To everything there is a season..

A time to live…
to breathe in the aroma of life
to pulsate as the heart beats
to hear the quiet sounds of nature
to savor with relish the harvest of earth
to freely drink of the nectar of life
to feel the wonders of the elements and
to gaze in awe at the beauties of creation.

A time to love…
to tenderly care for those we hold dear
to dare to hope
to show acts of benevolence
to laugh and cry with emotion
to manifest brotherly kindness
to give of ourselves
to envy not and
to be charitable and have compassion.

Love, Laughter And Living

A time to learn…
to read, study, and think
to speak and to listen
to make choices and wise decisions
to question and to seek answers
to positively expand our knowledge
to remember the good, forget the bad and
to realize the briefness of life and
the brevity of the season.

Joan Pace Kennedy

The Emergence of Spring

It's hard to be patient
With the prospect of new life
Anticipation builds up to a fever
Like expectant fathers – anxious
In a crowded waiting room.

Winter is long in labor
The fertile earth
With dormant seeds
Nurtured in the warmth of her womb
At last gives birth to virile green shoots.

Though not without pain
Does spring finally arrive
But, with cracking of the soil
Bursting of buds into fragrant blooms and
Writhing of tender branches.

Behold…
Life expelled from within.

Spring

Back in the woods along the stream
    Its banks covered in velvet green
      Water gently flowing
      Breezes quietly blowing
Creating an atmosphere serene.

Birds singing sweetly from the sky
    Joined in flight by the butterfly
      Buzzing bees
      And budding trees
Proclaim that spring is nigh.

The sun-warmed earth puts forth new shoots
    In the form of flowers, leaves, and roots
      The grass so green
      Completes the scene
Of a glimpse into nature's fruits.

Spring has knocked and nature has answered
    With oh, such beauty not yet heard
      Warm April showers
      Bring forth bright flowers,
Rainbows and the strain of birds.

Joan Pace Kennedy

Man responds to nature's call
In answer to spring's proclamation
With fishing poles
And kites so bold
He joins in the warm celebration.

Love, Laughter And Living

Golden Autumn

Autumn fires caught in the trees
Tinges of scarlet, purple, and scorched brown
Burn on the horizon
As far as the eye can see.

Trees dressed in autumn colors
A patchwork of crimson and gold
Prepared for the season
But all too soon to be undressed by winter's cold.

That first fall morning
The cool, crisp air
Rattles the dry, wrinkled leaves on the trees
Gently nudging, inviting, and then insisting that they fall.

The colorful collage of geometric design
Drifts unchartered in vivid descent
Leaving the trees bare, exposed
Naked skeletons of trunks and limbs.

The fall foliage, once scarlet and russet
Like gold at the end of the summer rainbow
The jagged patterns, profusion of colors
Now amber autumn leaves blanketing the ground.

Joan Pace Kennedy

Father's Day Tribute

Many years we've been together
Hand in hand, side by side
You've been my darling husband
Made me your happy bride.

You fathered our four children
My heart just swells with pride
I love you more each passing day
With you always abide.

Our children not only adore their dad
They respect and learn from you
So, on Father's Day I pledge my love
And your children honor you!

At our offspring, I now look
And ask, what do I see
Mirror images of their dad
They don't look at all like me.

Oh, they're just like their daddy
Folks remark most every day
Want to know a little secret?
I wouldn't have it any other way!

What is Happiness?

Happiness is a volatile emotion
Exploding peals of laughter
Chuckles, giggles, shouts of glee
Bursting forth with radiant smiles.

Happiness is a pendulum swinging from
    The satisfied norm to the ecstatic extreme
        Stretching out to either side
Its glowing touch far-reaching.

Happiness is a carnival carousel
That which goes around, comes around
A jolly merry-go-round
    Surviving in a circle of ups and downs.

Happiness is a rainbow of colors
    Arching up, bending low
        Apple red, sky blue,
Sunshine yellow, plum purple.

Happiness is a state of mind
That private, personal peace
Quiet, inner solace
Without an audible sound.

Joan Pace Kennedy

Finally Friday

Mr. Sun wasn't gentle as he pushed in
With sharp, piercing beams I was forced out
   Of that soft feather bed onto the hardwood floor.

Up the hall, down the steps, into the truck outside
   Then over the hills and under the Interstate
I rolled along to another day at the mill.

Inside, outside, upside down; that's how I feel
   As my world and work goes round in a spin
Day's made, I clock out, and start another regime.

Exhausted I exit, but soon refreshed I emerge
Prepared for whatever the night holds in store
For a willing soul ready to explore and discover.

Night, the flip side of the twelve hour day,
   All dressed up, headed downtown for the evening
   No clocking in, just checking out.

Clouds Like...

Wisps of curling smoke
Puffs of palpable cotton
Mounds of milky vapor
Hazy ghostly apparitions.

Dips and peaks of meringue
Swells of billowing snow
Heaps of mashed potatoes
Scoops of vanilla ice cream.

Rises of light, breezy feathers
Piles of shaving foam
Masses of bathing bubbles
Heavenly surfboards roam.

Sliding, drifting vapor
Swirls of whipped up cream
Curtains of filmy gauze
Transparent shreds of tissue.

Islands of white, now floating
In a beautiful sea of blue
Slow moving, inching icebergs
Stretched and tangled angel hair.

Joan Pace Kennedy

Relaxation

Take time to sit beneath the trees
To feel the cool and gentle breeze;
  Close your eyes and drift away,
  Forget the cares of every day
As you drift on cloudy seas.

Relax as wind blows through your hair
Taking with it worries and care
As you gently sway to the melody
  Played out by feathered friends.
Imagine your fantasies with dramatic flair.

Dare to dream of distant goals
Of sought after expectations
  Set for yourself in bygone days.
Construct your many dreams
Build castles because anything is possible.

Love, Laughter And Living

Rain

From whence did you ever
Conform, come together
To create the sprinkles,
The downpour, the storm.

Droplets, like crystal pebbles
Litter the walk, shower the grass
The roof, the body, and then again
Cascade into some unseen ravine.

Raindrops dancing, wet the panes
Slip across the window, sliding
Playing on the rain-dribbled glass
Rush to meet one another, colliding.

Wet together in spattering force
Agitate gently, wash away silt
From any form or shape that moves
From any structures built…

Ripples of rain – Running,
                Racing,
                      Receding.

Raindrops

Listen to the rhythm of the rain beat falling
    Pitter-patter, soft pebble sounds
    Gentle sprinkles, pounding drops
Rain comes spattering down all around.

    Drizzling rain trickling downward
        Gently nipping at the skin
            Torrents of rain seeking the ground
    Leave the rooftops glistening.

Steady droplets cause the showers
        Driving rain creates the storms
        Silver raindrops falling lightly
All are part of nature's forms.

Love, Laughter And Living

Summer Showers

When the land is parched, thirsty for drink
The skies are heavy and gray
Nature declares it won't be long
Until refreshing rain is on its way.

The immense blue sky opens wide her arms
Pours out the tears of her soul.
The miraculous drops of precipitation
Wake the dormant crops below.

Precious commodity, reviving rain
That liquid sunshine from the sky
Its moisture giving the earth new life
Adding spark and vitality to the living.

Cool showers make fresh the atmosphere
The crisp, clean smell that lingers.
The rustle of leaves as they swirl and sparkle
Are lit with dew, spilled from the heavens.

Sunlight breaks, streaming through the clouds
Steamy film rises from streets below.
A rainbow is painted across the sky
Earth refreshed, gives off a sigh.

Joan Pace Kennedy

Rainbow of Colors

We are a rainbow of colors
A star aglow with hues
Blue, yellow, white, green, red.
In our garden of flowers
Just as flowers differ
So do individual personalities.

Each one holds its own beauty
But singles become lovelier
When the stems are brought together
To form a colorful bouquet.

Then, like colors of the rainbow
We, too, should arch ever upward
And let our "colors" proudly show
Focusing our star points aloft
Striving for the best each and every year.

The beautiful blue is a sign
of loyalty, faithfulness, and fidelity.
Yellow is a sign of glowing energy
of zeal, and of confidence.
The white symbolizes honesty
purity, and innocence.

Love, Laughter And Living

Green is symbolic of the freshness of life
of birth, and of new growth.
The radiant red stands for fervent love
courage, and bravery.

Now as each color comes together
let us unite and be as loving
to one another in our bouquet of life
as these flowers are beautiful
when they are joined in a vase.

Joan Pace Kennedy

Nature's Palette

   Sparks of color, splashes of hue
        Fragrant flowers, budding blooms
        Blossoms curled, wispy with dew
  Radiate, saturate, and permeate.

    The omnipotent gardener
          With multi-color palette
        Paints leaves, stalks, and petals
  Creating a masterpiece design.

  Picture perfect buds and blossoms
Spindly stalks, stumps, and limbs
Litter the land, halo the hillside
    And daringly drape the ditches.

    As if the waving of a magic wand
          Has turned the dreary roadways
          Into bright and cheery byways
  Glowing in vast array, a cache of color.

  Glorious rainbows, tints, and shades
  Bulbs, blades, clusters, and sprays
  Freshly snipped buds, a spreading bouquet
Speak to our spirit, our senses, and emotions.

Dancing gracefully in a lively scene
    Their luring beauty around the globe
    The mystery of flowers remains to be seen
Their value quite obvious around the world.

Floral arrangements, geometric design
    A haze of beauty, bountiful at birth
    Cascading buds in wedding bouquets
Funeral wreaths and casket sprays.

Flowers preserved in memory mellow
Of treasured times, in mind recesses
    Sights and smells of petals surrounding
Leaves unfolding spread open wide.

Plants and flowers have ever survived
    A glimpse into nature's fragrant expressions
Lovely flowers preserved in a vase
Splayed out on canvas for the world to gaze.

After they have dried…petals and leaves shed
    Long after they are gone, withered and limp
    The memory of blossoms remains in our head
Before us, there for us, and even on after us.

Optimism

Oh, life's a bowl of cherries
Sometimes juicy and red.
But, remember there are the pits
Or so it has been said.

As roses grow along the thorns
    And tares among the wheat
    Life's happenings come sour
They are mingled with the sweet.

Don't be discouraged when bad luck
    Is seen standing at your door.
    Get out your broom and sweep him off
Set sight for something more.

For when it seems you're down and out
Remember this one thing
    The only way from down is up
    So lift your head and sing.

Without the valleys, there are no hills
    Never a mountain peak.
        Grey skies have a silver lining
    And the darkness a shining streak.

The Sun

From the pink glow of blushing sunrise
To the red glare of blazing sunset
This fiery ball arches the sky
Giving light and supplying warmth
Providing a guiding orb.

No one has ever ventured near
This dynamic sphere of molten gas
Too fervent, this brilliant devouring element
None can conquer or change her ways.
She rules with a firm and mighty hand.

Were we only able to tame her wilds
Channel that abundant mass of energy
Find ways to tap such a powerful source
Ease the energy crisis here on earth and
Make use of this solar almighty.

Gleaming star that lightens the day
Supreme as she reigns in the heavens
Radiant beauty, fulfilling her role
Penetrating the earth with her flaming gaze
Warming the sod and nurturing life.

Joan Pace Kennedy

Sunshine

The sun streaming through branches
Creating ribbons of light
Playing on sidewalks
Casting shadows.

Bright beams peering through clouds
Bouncing from walls
Dancing on rocks
Reflecting moisture.

Narrow glints of piercing sun
Slicing the sky
Shafts of light
Spewing downward.

Sparkling rays of golden glimmer
Enveloping the flowers
Kissing the earth
Nurturing life.

Love, Laughter And Living

Day vs. Night

That slit of light between earth and sky
A glimpse of meringue topped cherry pie.

As daylight departs to make way for night
The canvas above is a beautiful sight.

Painted with tinges of scarlet and gold
Colors cascading in pleats and folds.

Clouds and sun give way, as is right
But in their passing, put up a good fight.

Clashing elements, night against day
Leave conflicting heavens the price to pay.

Strong, vibrant smears, but fading fast
Day stands suspended, but succumbs at last.

Joan Pace Kennedy

Christmas

It's the season of peace, of hope, and joy
A time of sharing and giving
But alas, the days go whirling by
    There is barely time for living.

We hurry to work and rush to leave
    Searching for gifts and décor
Then, when we think we've finally finished
    We discover we need just one more.

Christmas comes but once a year
    The season of Jesus' birth
    To celebrate the sacred time
God sent his Son to earth.

Yet, we're so filled with monetary thoughts
We've become too commercialized
And we often leave out the Lord
    On Christmas, right before our eyes.

Let us not concentrate on the earthly theme
    But, lift up our voice in praise
To celebrate our precious Savior's birth
And spread joy throughout these days.

Chapter 7
Along The Way

Sack of Socks for St. Jude
The Word Not Spoken
Life's Long Highway
The Novel of Life
Leaving a Legacy
The Face
Heartbreak
End of Day, End of Play
Theater of Life
Dreadful Decision
Death
Last Request
Untimely Death
Changing Pace
Thoughts on Life
Shoes, Shoes, and More Shoes
Unfinished Goals
Man's Race with Time
Life Is
Fleeting Days
Brother Lochte and the Lord
Your Name

Joan Pace Kennedy

Sack of Socks for St. Jude

For the little feet who wait to greet
the doctor of the day
For the toes that wiggle in anticipation
of what he's going to say.
For the feet of the child who has to face
another day of fear
Of the diagnosis, the prognosis
and what he is going to hear.

These socks are sent to lift the spirits
of the little ones already there
To make those feet become happy feet
these socks from us we share.
We send them with love, with prayers
and hope, for longer days of ease
All kinds of socks, silly socks
to "sock it" to each disease.

So from us to you, this message we send
along with our sack of socks
Socks of color, socks of design,
socks for the long and short.
All for the feet, the ten little toes
socks with tassels or blends
To remind you that you're not forgotten
but remembered by many friends.

The Word Not Spoken

Lines from Frost in "The Road Not Taken"
Cause one to ponder the journey of our words.
Some words are uttered, some yelled, or whispered
But what of the words not spoken?

What of good deeds, the gestures that bind
Fine fortunes to us…friends, family and kin.
Did comments like "Thanks" or "Appreciation"
To your mind, immediately, enter in?

Many words not spoken leave behind a void
Some emptiness, a sadness, or blind to those
Whose lives might be changed by such words
Syllables not spoken would be rich, if heard.

Words left unspoken, unuttered, unsaid
Are bouquets of blossoms…undelivered, unread.
So, choose your road, take it; scatter words as you go
Leave nothing to chance, let those flowers grow!

Life's Long Highway

Life's long highway has many a turn
The more you think you know
The more you have to learn.

Traveling life's highway, a twist then a turn
Deep chasms to cross
And some bridges to burn.

Feelings get hurt from words angrily thrown
Folks you thought you knew
Emerge as never you've known.

They smile to your face; then stab from behind
With festered words of hatred
What provoked them to be so unkind?

Life's highway of circles continues its bends
That which rolls round and round
Will surely come round again.

Life's truly a highway; you'll have ups and downs
Each day will be different
You'll laugh, cry, or frown.

Joan Pace Kennedy

But life will go on, even after you're gone
So leave footprints to follow
For someone to tread on.

The Novel of Life

The cover opens and we emerge
Ready to enter the novel of life
The contents page…our own timeline
Includes the phases, the chapters.

Chapter one…we're born, we breathe
    In chapter two we continue to grow
    Chapter three sees us go to school
And oh, the things we get to know.

Chapter four brings us through our teens
Filled with turmoil, change, and dreams
Visions of grandeur, plans aplenty
  But, before we know it, we turn twenty.

    Chapter five, the teen years gone
        College or trade; marriage or home
        Earning a living, making a life
Perhaps someone's husband, maybe a wife.

  Chapter six presents this book's midway
      Middle age, maturity…it came on so fast
    Chapter seven sees change, kids leave the nest
Facing old age, striving to do your best.

Joan Pace Kennedy

To live Chapter eight, with its aches and pains
Is a challenge in itself, don't mean to complain
But as Chapter nine opens, life's nearly spent
    And you now realize how swiftly it went.

    Chapter ten brings us to the end of the book
        In recollection and recall, when we take a look
    It was quite a story, this blessed life of mine
    So now all that's left is the end of time.

Leaving a Legacy

We all leave footprints wherever we go
Somebody will follow our heel and our toe.
Which way do we walk, is it a determined gait,
Do we follow a path or explore until late?

Are we aware of the scenes as we travel along?
Are our footprints accompanied by laughter and song?
The footprints we leave may be crooked or straight,
Go directly to our destination or meander by a lake.

Agendas determine which way we will walk
And footprints leave messages as sure as our talk.
The direction we traveled, the traipse of our shoe
Can be seen by those following our trail's avenue.

Our footprints tell much of how we travel in life
Where we go, what we do, where we've been is a sight.
Make sure that your footprints lead straight and for right
Have courage to lead in the pathway of light.

Strive for your dreams, let your footprints lead high.
Then when you reach the pinnacle,
you can smile as you sigh
Looking back down the path from whence you have come,
Surveying all the footprints and the tasks that you've done.

Lessons are learned from sheer observation
Footprints testify of perseverance and obligation.
Footprints reflect who we are, what we've done
Footprints left for others show the way that we've run.

The Face

The glaring face peers out into dead darkness
Bearing witness to the ungodly hour
Hands silently sweep the orb
Swiftly if unheeded, slowly if watched.

Suddenly awakened, eyes are drawn
To that number ridden screen
An instant message seers the brain
As we pay homage to that alarming face.

Time – played out like a musical score
This familiar face and fleeting hands
Perform measure to measure, minute to minute
As the hours consume the days.

A dependent facial feature
Traveling companion, steady and sure
Marks the steps from day to day
Gives order and direction to cluttered life.

Heartbreak

It is over and done with, by now she is gone
And you sit here crying so blue and alone.
Consumed with the feeling of being lonesome
As the D.J. continues those sad, dismal songs.

Her leaving was what you thought you'd never see
Single is not all it is cracked up to be.
Missing her changes the meaning of freedom
As the radio blares out those heartbreaking songs.

End of Day, End of Play

Another night falling at the end of the day
A dropped curtain signals the end of the play
    Acts performed on earth or on stage
Leave behind memories that linger through age.

Darkness envelopes as curtains roll down
Unfolding to close out the sights and sounds
Of the played-out scenes that are all now past
    Act I, Act II, they've gone by so fast.

Soon the dawn will open Act III with the light
    Gone then the darkness of the shadowed night
A final appearance, rendition complete
Then the character is gone, audience on its feet

To exhort, extol, or condemn what was done
    On the stage, in the life, in the dark, in the sun
Of such are the memories that linger in time
Called forth now and then to savor like wine.

Love, Laughter And Living

Theater of Life

When I open my eyes to a new beginning
The birth of a sparkling new day
Who knows what waits on the vast horizon
What song or dance or character will play.

Each day the stage is different
When the curtain on life is drawn
And the parts assigned go to men of all kind
Unfolding like petals at dawn.

With the world as our public theater
We choose carefully how we will act
With a lifetime of rehearsal and practice
We perform life's spectacle intact.

We must play the part we're given
Accountable to the very end
Be true to ourselves and to others
For who knows what lies around the bend.

Each day we live and strive to build
Characters to withstand the fall
But the acts of our plays are passing
The final curtain descends on us all.

Joan Pace Kennedy

We all have a choice in how to act
In our own special way – unique
Our ability, freedom, and action in creating
The character that we choose to be.

Dreadful Decision

With no forethought, he accepted the drugs
along with the drink, looking for a thrill
a means of escape from the daily routine
the lonely boredom of his life.

Without a question or doubt
he sought a way out
of his everyday monotony.

Surrounded by peers, he felt the need
to conform to their easy lifestyle.
Faced by temptations numerous times before
tonight he surrendered, hesitated no more.

With no thought for tomorrow
he partook in their pleasure
not seeing the end
of this disastrous measure.

Self-involvement or peer acceptance
blinded by misunderstanding
with continued use, he lay the foundation
for self-destruction through substance abuse.

Joan Pace Kennedy

Death

Death, that unwelcome stranger
   Sneaking in like a thief
      Unexpected, unforeseen, suddenly
      Stealing a precious loved one.

          Death, so final and absolute
      No option to turn back
      Unannounced and overpowering
      Erasing life away.

Death, the entrance to the unknown
      The world beyond, another dimension
         Relinquishing all earthly ties
   Separating the body and the soul.

Death, uncompromising in execution
Shrewd, cunning, master of the game
Like the closing of a curtain
   Between what was and what will never be.

   Death, with a cloak of darkness
      Shrouded in mystery, stalking its prey
         All mankind is eventually conquered
   No barrier hinders as each succumbs.

Last Request

If I should die tomorrow
         Don't morn my passing away
      Though brief this earthly journey
The life was rich and bountiful.

If I should die tomorrow
         Don't weep or cry for me
      For I have gone, to my heavenly home,
To sing praises to our King.

If I should die tomorrow
         Don't be sad or shed a tear
Just smile as you remember me
And pledge up there we'll meet.

      If I should die tomorrow
         Do not fret or be forlorn
      Think about how we loved in life
And give thanks for whatever comes.

If I should die tomorrow
I had a full and happy life
      I loved it and lived it to the fullest
I have been truly blessed.

Joan Pace Kennedy

Untimely Death

Come quick, she said…to the hospital with haste
    He's in the ER; there is no time to waste.
Without knowing details, I sped off toward town
Echoing warnings of be careful and slow down.

    Arrived in the middle of chaos and tears
        Folks standing around with faces of fear.
    Mingled, muffled voices with a hush in the midst
The family's in anguish, what a tragic twist.

    In a very short time, it was evident to see
        That this was a critical…e-mer-gen-cy.
        No pulse, no heartbeat, but shocked back to life
Surrounded by children and a grieving wife.

No visible response, lying helpless and still
    Doctors worked feverishly, signs of life to feel.
        It was hard to think straight, emotions awhirl
Not knowing the future of their little world.

    Friends reached out, rushed in as they were
        Some came half dressed, but what did they care.
This was one of their own, in trouble for sure
They showed love and respect, they prayed for a cure.

Love, Laughter And Living

We've done all we can, for survival we grope
But there's still a slim chance, now go with that hope.
The ambulance is waiting to transfer him soon
But the doctors must stabilize before they can move.

With lights flashing red, and attendants in place
Children and wife followed as they tried to keep pace.
It seemed like forever, but they finally were there
Whisked into the ICU, for infinite care.

The hours dragged by, the night lay dark and long
In the waiting room we huddled,
                         talked and answered the phone.
Morning news was no better, doctors talked very plain
They said there's little hope now that he will remain.

So this family of three and their minister too
Along with the nurse, stood watch and they knew
That the time had come, when they had to let him go
And after prayers and good-byes, they softly told him so.

You've been a good husband and a wonderful dad
A friend to so many who were heartbroken and sad.
The small group talked on, showed love and sang songs
Until he was lifted with prayers to his final home.

Joan Pace Kennedy

Changing Pace

Worldly goods and earthly fame,
We strive toward with might.
Through thick and thin,
With foe and friend,
We won't give up the fight.

Day in, day out, our whole life through
We work and plan ahead.
Blind fury fills each hour
Of the race in search of power
Making some days dawn with dread.

Is there some way to change the tide,
Be master of the game?
Confront the uncertain,
Shed life's heavy burdens
Achieving our goals just the same.

Slow down the wheels that turn the clock,
Be more involved and alive.
Take time to play
Find happiness each day
So the good times will survive.

Love, Laughter And Living

    For the chance of life comes only once
          To all the human race.
              Grab hold of the ring
                      As you whistle and sing
            And much of the strain you'll erase.

Joan Pace Kennedy

Thoughts on Life

Life is a journey...
A trip across the aeons of time
The trip is long and tedious
An incessant battle and struggle for survival
A constant war combating the realities of life
And the conflict never ends until
Death becomes the conqueror.

Life is a sport...
A competition to be met head-on
Adhering to the rules does not always ensure victory
But, how the game is played,
knowing you did your best
Can alleviate inner turmoil and
bring about peace within
Then, upon reflection of the game,
you can say with pride
It was well worth the effort.

Life is a challenge...
A dare to be all that you can be
Opportunity reaches out to beckon
But, you must venture forth to accept the invitation

Love, Laughter And Living

The challenge waits like an open double door
                Step forward boldly to enter
            Embark on the journey of life.

Joan Pace Kennedy

Shoes, Shoes, and More Shoes

Brand new shoes that sparkle and shine
Pretty new shoes on these feet of mine.
Shown in the window, sitting on the shelf
Shoes for babies, for moms, and myself.

Work shoes, dress shoes, even strappy mesh shoes.
Genuine leather or man created, we choose
The shoes to cover our feet, our ten little toes.
Slip on our choice shoes to match our clothes.

Nomadic shoes that traveled many long miles
Shoes that have brought forth smile after smile.
Devoid of shoes, our feet would be bare
Just look at these shoes, we all have a pair.

Old worn-out shoes cast off, cast aside
Scuffed and dirty, worn no more with pride.
Shoes with thin soles, yet resoled with care
Weathered shoes from much wear and tear.

Tennis shoes or boots, sandals or high heels
We all wear shoes for their comfortable feel.
Our favorites, when shabby, we dread to surrender
These shoes we will cling to and always remember.

Love, Laughter And Living

Unfinished Goals

There are so many things I'd like to do
So many missions to accomplish
Before this life is through.

Scenes to paint and films to see
Museums to browse, books to read
Things out there, yet to be.

Songs to sing and music to hear
Poetry that stirs the soul
Beats to chant and cheer.

Trying to seize just a little bit more
Of happiness, laughter, and love
I want ALL of what life holds in store.

It seems so brief, it goes by too fast
We're born, grow up, grow old, and die
Knowing that nothing will last.

So with this in mind, I'll do my best
To take one day at a time
Live life to the fullest and give my love
To each and every one of mine.

Joan Pace Kennedy

Man's Race with Time

Sunrise and the new day begins
The sun emerges like glowing embers
As a quiet, newborn babe
Peaceful at its mother's breast
So the sun lies close to the earth on the horizon.
Morning brings the sun up into the sky
Rising and stretching toward new heights
Much as a teen longs to reach out and
pursue goals and dreams
With youthful drive and passion
Advancing steadily with enthusiasm.
High Noon finds the sun standing straight overhead
Tall as a young man reaching adulthood
Looking back from whence he came
Gazing into the unknown future
Yet knowing, all the while, that right now
he is at his peak.
Afternoon begins the descent of the sun
The gradual slowing down of motion
The moderate change of pace
Tardy, leisurely, and deliberate steps
Bring the day to a close.

Love, Laughter And Living

Sunset and the day merges into darkness as
The sun unites once more with the earth
The same as man who from dust was formed
And to dust will return
The day is done and man's race is run.

Joan Pace Kennedy

Life Is...

Life is a breath
What we take in is what we'll give out

Life is a whisper
Listen carefully or you'll miss something

Life is a dialogue
Be careful what you say, how you reply

Life is a prayer
A talk with the Master starts the day right

Life is a conference
Making plans, decisions, concessions

Life is a joke
Surely you jest, it's not a picnic, but…smile

Life is a celebration
A party of sorts, a fair, a carnival festival

Life is a song
Melodies high and low, the cadence fast and slow

Love, Laughter And Living

Life is a convention
A dialogue between challenges and achievements

Life is a sport
A game, a challenge, a competition

Life is a journey
Winding roads, high mountains and deep valleys

Life is a struggle
Filled with sorrow, grief, and tears

Life is a gamble
A chance at the big time or risk at failure.

Fleeting Days

As time rolls on and we grow old
Life does take on new meaning
Childhood blooms into bright youth
Speeding without rhyme or reason.

And down life's road amid the pain
                    We struggle for survival
          Trying to accomplish noble deeds
             That lead us to our horizons.

We set our goals and strive toward
Some end that soars to heights
  Unscaled by those who failed to get
    Their name up in the lights.

    Is this what life is all about
    The rush, the push, and shove?
      Can't we slow down and smell the flowers
And share life with those we love.

Love, Laughter And Living

Brother Lochte and the Lord

Long ago in thirty-seven
A young man heeded the call
To follow the Lord in service
Spread the gospel to one and all.

The road was not always easy
Sometimes the going was slow
But all the while God was with him
Sustained his needs and blessed him so.

It wasn't the words of the country boy
But the Lord who spoke from within
When he preached the message loud and clear
Convicting lost souls to be saved from sin.

With God as his guide, Mrs. Wilda his bride
This trio touched many a heart
Years on the field for Jesus Christ
Salvation to impart.

Joan Pace Kennedy

Your Name

You're born with a name,
from where did it come?
You're your parents' daughter
or you are their son.

You're born with a name,
whether you like it or not.
You were given that name
by your mom and pop.

You're born with a name,
you carry through life.
It's always the same,
until you're a wife.

You're born with a name,
wear it with pride.
For a chosen good name,
you should always strive.

You're born with a name,
yours until you die.
Be proud of that name
and hold your head high.

Love, Laughter And Living

We all have a choice in how to act
In our own special way – unique
Our ability, freedom, and action in creating
The character that we choose to be.

Joan Pace Kennedy

Love, Laughter And Living

www.ingramcontent.com/pod-product-compliance
Lightning Source LLC
Chambersburg PA
CBHW071732080526
44588CB00013B/1993